"Tired of feeling frustrated? Starting to feel like it's hopeless? Don't waste another minute: read this book, get inspired, and maximize your effectiveness!"

—**Jon Bockman**, Executive Director
Animal Charity Evaluators

"Matt Ball is a thought leader in the animal movement who has helped pave an important path towards more pragmatic advocacy. For years he's inspired many not to focus on activism that may "feel good," but rather on what's actually effective."

—**Erica Meier**, Executive Director
Compassion Over Killing

"Matt Ball presents activists with the most important question: How can I do the most good? His essays are required reading for all our staff and interns."

—**David Coman-Hidy**
Executive Director, The Humane League

"Matt Ball is the activist's activist. His mantra is effectiveness; his style is cool, calm, and collected; and his driving force is a palpable passion to end suffering. If you want to find out how to make your life matter, this collection of his wisdom is necessary reading."

—**Jasmin Singer** and **Mariann Sullivan**
Our Hen House

"There are few people whose work I have more respect and admiration for than Matt Ball. A true pioneer, Matt has put veganism on the map, sparing millions of animals from suffering on factory farms. I am excited that this book exists and hope it will serve as a textbook for new and veteran advocates alike."

—**Kristie Middleton**, Food Policy Manager
The Humane Society of the United States

"I highly recommend *The Accidental Activist* for all of us who strive to become more effective voices for animals."

—**Josh Balk**, Director of Food Policy
The Humane Society of the United States

"For over two decades Matt Ball has shaped, led, and expanded vegan advocacy. He's shared a wealth of information over these years, never hesitating to examine and modify his own assumptions and strategies as he went. *The Accidental Activist* highlights the best of his work, with the added bonus of pieces by other leaders in the movement whom he's inspired. Read it and be inspired, too."

—**Charlie Talbert**, Board President
Alliance For Animals and the Environment

"Read this book if you want to prevent cruelty and inspire compassion." —**Nathan Runkle**
Executive Director, Mercy for Animals

"Animal advocates are fortunate to have the benefit of Matt Ball's many years of experience as an activist, and to be able to access that experience through his writing. In his essays, Matt provides many important insights and guidance for anyone who wishes to wield their time and resources to efficiently defend animals from harm."

—**Mark Middleton**, AnimalVisuals

"Matt Ball is one of my heroes. There is nothing I want more than to help make the world a kinder place, and nobody whose work has guided me better toward that goal. This book is a terrific collection of his ideas. I recommend wholeheartedly that it go to the very top of every activist's reading list."

—**Karen Dawn**, DawnWatch
and author of *Thanking the Monkey*

THE ACCIDENTAL ACTIVIST

Stories, Speeches, Articles, and Interviews by Vegan Outreach's Cofounder

MATT BALL

Foreword by Peter Singer
Introduction by Paul Shapiro
Edited by Anne Green, Ph.D.

With Joe Espinosa, Ellen Green, Ginny Messina R.D., John Oberg, Dawn Ratcliffe, Harish Sethu, Vic Sjodin, Stewart Solomon, and Kenny Torrella.

TheAccidentalActivist.net

LANTERN BOOKS · NEW YORK
A Division of Booklight Inc.

2014
Lantern Books
128 Second Place
Brooklyn, NY 11231
www.lanternbooks.com

Printed in the United States of America

ISBN (pbk) 978-1-59056-454-7, (e) 978-1-59056-455-4
Library of Congress CIP information is available.

Contents

I. LEARNING CURVE   1

II. BEING VEGAN   57

IV. FOCUS 179

V. THE FUTURE 225

Foreword

Peter Singer

I have followed Matt Ball and Vegan Outreach's evolution for many years, and observed the parallels with the evolution of the animal rights movement in the United States. Matt began his involvement in animal rights in the 1980s by participating in, and sometimes getting arrested during, protests against the use of fur, and against testing household products on animals.

Nowadays, Matt, in keeping with a large proportion of current animal activists, is much more focused on utilitarian goals—remembering, of course, that utilitarians such as Jeremy Bentham, John Stuart Mill, and Henry Sidgwick were always careful to include the welfare of animals, along with that of humans, when speaking of reducing pain and suffering. The bottom line for Matt is to have the greatest possible beneficial impact for animals, given the finite resources available. Matt's advocacy is informed by his understanding of psychology and the social sciences. It is based on a realistic, thorough, and ongoing evaluation of society as it currently is, and on how change can and does come about at different levels, from individuals to industries.

The consequences of this significant shift in the efforts of so many activists are evident. The movement to reduce animal suffering is having an impact, and the extent of that impact is growing at an accelerating pace. More people are changing their diet and eating fewer animals. More importantly, the number of animals killed in the United States is in decline, even as the population grows. A new future is in sight, one that Matt, Vegan Outreach, and other advocates are hard at work creating.

There is room for diverse views within the animal movement. Not every animal activist will agree with Matt on the best focus for her or his activities, nor on the best way of reducing animal suffering. Nevertheless, every activist will benefit from reading about how Matt arrived at where he is today—especially because he is candid in describing what he now considers mistakes and missteps. Wisdom is the ability to learn from one's mistakes and from the mistakes of others. We are fortunate to have people like Matt helping us to be wiser tomorrow.

December 2013

Introduction

Paul Shapiro
Vice President, Farm Animal Protection
The Humane Society of the United States

I have a confession. As with most confessions, it's one I'm not proud of. And, perhaps unlike most things an animal advocate would confess, it harmed animals.

Before I get there, let me tell you a little about myself. I became vegan in 1993 and have devoted much of my time since then to trying to give animals a voice and reducing their suffering. I founded an animal protection club in high school called Compassion Over Killing, which later became a national organization. After ten years of running that organization, I left to work at the world's largest animal protection organization, The Humane Society of the United States, where I now serve as vice president of farm animal protection.

During these past two decades, I've been a part of dozens of campaigns: political campaigns, corporate campaigns, outreach and awareness campaigns, and more. The driving question in my life is a simple one: How can I most effectively be an ambassador for animals and therefore reduce the greatest amount of suffering?

But it wasn't always that way. It wasn't always the case that effectiveness came first in my mind. You see, when I first became involved in animal protection, I suffered from what some people jokingly call "newveganitis." As a young teen, I was sometimes more focused on what made me feel good, what made me feel right, what made me feel "pure" when it came to these serious issues. Effectiveness, I'm ashamed to admit, sometimes sat lonely in the back seat.

So here's my confession: I believe that much of what I did in the first several years of my life as an animal advocate didn't do that much to help animals. In fact, the real confession is that some of it was actually counterproductive, meaning I believe it harmed animals.

Fortunately for me, and even more fortunately for animals, reading one of Matt Ball's essays (a precursor to "A Meaningful Life") changed so many of my views on animal advocacy.

I wasn't short on desire to help animals. I wasn't short on repulsion at animal cruelty. I wasn't short on willingness to make sacrifices to try to advance animals' interests. What I was short on was the type of strategic pragmatism that Matt opened me up to.

Matt made it clear that the bottom line in animal advocacy is how much suffering we can reduce (and, of course, creating happiness is also very important). Everything else, as they say, is just commentary.

My appearance was once one that was, let's just say, countercultural. At one time, multiple earrings adorned my lobes, dreadlocks fell from my scalp, and a long wallet chain hung from my very oversized jeans. I was the type of person who would implore myself and my fellow animal advocates to be willing to do almost anything for animals, which of course makes sense, considering the unfathomable misery our species inflicts upon them.

I remember imploring other advocates to shout our lungs out for animals, to argue with people and try to "beat them" in those arguments, and so on. It was even common back then just to expect as an a priori assumption that "true" animal advocates would be willing to go to jail without question "for the animals."

The painful questions I wasn't asking included the following: Was I willing to get a haircut for animals? Was I willing to put on a button-down shirt for animals? More broadly, was I willing to actually try to be effective for animals?

Rather than being interested in winning arguments and being right, I needed to be more interested in winning people over and being effective. For animals, it's not enough for us to be right. We need to be both right and effective.

Matt's essay caused me to rethink my focus on animal advocacy: to concentrate primarily on farm animals since they represent the vast majority of all the animals we exploit; to modify my own appearance so it would no longer be a stumbling block for others to dismiss compassionate living; to recognize that we tend to accomplish more with a friendly, welcoming message than one which simply accuses and condemns.

I recall stupidly thinking when I was a new vegan that in advocating dietary change, it was all or nothing. Of course, I now recognize that countless people care about animals and want to help them, but they may not be ready to become vegan. We should be welcoming to everyone who wants to help animals, no matter where they are on their journey. That's not to say we shouldn't always encourage continuous improvement for everyone—myself certainly included—but it is to say that there shouldn't be an orthodoxy or litmus test for people wanting to do something helpful for animals.

In many ways, it boils down to this question: Do we want a social club, or do we want a social movement? If we want a social movement, we need to open our arms and have a big tent.

To be a big tent, it's imperative that we continually ask ourselves the following: Are we so insular as a movement that we demand purity rather than progress? Are we so orthodox that we don't applaud people for taking the first step, but rather punish them for not taking the last step?

By adopting a mentality that welcomes people where they are and applauds them for taking the steps they've taken, and by reminding ourselves in a friendly way that we should continually strive for uninterrupted improvement in those parts of the advocacy that matter most, our movement—and therefore animals—will be much better off.

I don't profess to have all, or even most, of the answers on how to be an effective animal advocate, and certainly neither does Matt. But I do know that I wish his essays had been around when I first became part of the animal protection movement. Perhaps I'd have a bit less to confess today had I been able to read them back then.

You don't have that excuse. You now have the benefit of reading Matt's essays right here, and then thinking critically about how they may help you become a more pragmatic protector of animals. I'm certain they'll give you a lot to think about, and, more importantly, to act on.

December 2013

Editor's Note

WARNING: Nonlinear—A Reader's Guide
to The Accidental Activist

Anne Green

During the twenty-one-plus years I've known Matt, I've heard him give many talks and be questioned by hundreds of people. I've read what seems like millions of words he's written, and I've edited some of the essays in this book many times over. I think it's reasonable to say I'm more familiar with Matt's way of thinking than anyone else.

Perhaps the most important thing to understand about Matt is that he doesn't deal in superficialities. He's always trying to find the crux of the issue and address the root. At his core, Matt is an engineer, and he seeks to understand the fundamentals in order to optimize the solution. Given his nature, Matt's writings and speeches focus on only a handful of topics. From these few basics, he derives specific conclusions, depending on the specific question.

For his first book, *The Animal Activist's Handbook*, Matt took his and Bruce Friedrich's essays and talks, broke them down, and rearranged them into a coherent, linear progression, with a very specific narrative arc. For

The Accidental Activist, however, I said he should do something different: Let those individual pieces stand alone, organized only by general topic.

Thus, it's my "fault" this book isn't linear. If you try to read it straight through, the repetition will almost certainly bore or frustrate you. (Sorry, Matt, but on your chosen topics, you can be like a dog with a vegan bone.) Furthermore, given that the essays aren't organized by date but rather jump around in time, it can be confusing to read something positive from 2010, then a crisis from the late 1990s, only to next come across a glowing, optimistic vision of the future from 2013.[1]

My strong advice, therefore, is don't read *The Accidental Activist* from beginning to end! Rather, choose based on which topic you're interested in at the moment, or by which chapter title sounds intriguing. Although these essays were never meant to be part of a single, coherent book, we at Vegan Outreach regularly hear from people whose lives have been changed by these essays. I am confident some will resonate with you, too.

January 2014

---

1 Throughout the book, the dates provided at the start of each piece generally refer to when the work first appeared or the talk was given.

I.

LEARNING CURVE

Belief on the Right Side of History

A Talk in Salt Lake City, Utah, 2012

Most people think a concern for animals is limited to liberals. But this isn't necessarily the case. Many Vegan Outreach leafleters report they were received more openly at places like Brigham Young and the University of Oklahoma than Berkeley or the University of Colorado in Boulder.

I am a good example as well. I was raised in a religious family and went to religious schools all the way through high school. I read Ayn Rand and considered myself a "neocon."

Three events changed my outlook.

The first occurred when I was in high school. An older cousin I had admired left our church and joined the Bahá'í religion. As nearly everyone I knew—my circle of friends, classmates—were of the same religion, I had hardly ever considered other religions; when I did, I thought of them as slightly "wrong" versions of Christianity. Yet here was a very different religion that led my cousin to leave the church of her upbringing. Obviously, my first reaction was to simply dismiss my cousin as misguided, and the Bahá'í religion as heresy. But in the back of my mind, I wondered.

The second event was studying World War II. (Growing up, I loved airplanes; WWII was the time of greatest change in aircraft.) I had always assumed the Holocaust was the work of just a few individuals. I discovered, though, that the Germans knew what was going on, and, except for a relatively small proportion of the population, supported it.

Like most Americans, I had always been horrified by slavery in our country. The idea of treating other people as mere property—and that so many people would fight and die for the "right" to do so—was both shocking and appalling. Simply and utterly bewildering.

But learning more about the Holocaust revealed an even worse aspect of human nature—where people turn on their fellow citizens, systematically and methodically exterminating them.

Obviously, the normal reaction is to assume that I would have been a part of the Underground Railroad, or would have protected the Anne Franks of the world. But . . . really? Did I honestly think I would have gone against the overwhelming majority of my society? If I had been raised in a slave-holding household in a slave-holding society, would I really have stood up? Was I truly different from everyone who viewed certain people as "property," who went along with Hitler's "Final Solution"?

Did I honestly think I would have been different from nearly everyone else?

And if all these millions could fully believe things that, today, are so obviously absurd and repulsive, how could I assume everything I currently believed was absolutely right? If so many would willingly support gruesome atrocities, how could I possibly think everything today is morally pure? Even if I'm not chaining up a slave or leading my fellow citizens to the gas chambers, isn't it possible—even probable—that I am at least tacitly supporting another horror, one that future generations will also look upon with bewilderment?

The answer came my first year of college, when I met my vegetarian roommate. Fred—a big block of a man—introduced me to the horrors of modern agribusiness. Again, I was not a liberal. I was a middle-class kid who dreamed of a successful career, a bigger house, a cool car, an elaborate stereo system, travel, and good food. That first week of college, my parents and I planned to celebrate my future graduation at the city's five-star French restaurant.

I didn't go vegetarian. As uncomfortable as Fred made me with his stories of how animals were treated on farms—the brandings, the debeakings, the tail dockings, the confinement—I justified eating animals by saying that they were "just animals."

But the stories did bother me. There's plenty of gruesome video footage to turn your stomach[1] (more is released every month), but I'd rather give a description from the *New York Times*[2]:

---

1 See the "Video Links" page on Vegan Outreach's Web site: www.veganoutreach.org/video. All links accessed January 2014.

2 Michael Pollan, "An Animal's Place," *New York Times*, November 10, 2002.

Piglets in confinement operations are weaned from their mothers [quickly] because they gain weight faster on their hormone- and antibiotic-fortified feed. This premature weaning leaves the pigs with a lifelong craving to suck and chew, a desire they gratify in confinement by biting the tail of the animal in front of them. A normal pig would fight off his molester, but a demoralized pig has stopped caring. "Learned helplessness" is the psychological term, and it's not uncommon in confinement operations, where tens of thousands of hogs spend their entire lives ignorant of sunshine or earth or straw, crowded together beneath a metal roof upon metal slats suspended over a manure pit. So it's not surprising that an animal as sensitive and intelligent as a pig would get depressed, and a depressed pig will allow his tail to be chewed on to the point of infection. Sick pigs, being underperforming "production units," are clubbed to death on the spot. The USDA's recommended solution to the problem is called "tail docking." Using a pair of pliers (and no anesthetic), most but not all of the tail . . . is snipped off. Why the little stump? Because the whole point of the exercise is not to remove the object of tail-biting so much as to render it more sensitive. Now, a bite on the tail is so painful that even the most demoralized pig will mount a struggle to avoid it.

And a different section:

The American laying hen . . . passes her brief span piled together with a half-dozen other hens in a wire cage whose floor a single page of this magazine could carpet. Every natural instinct of this animal is thwarted, leading to a range of behavioral "vices" that can include cannibalizing her cagemates and rubbing her body against the wire mesh until it is featherless and bleeding. . . . The [five percent] or so of hens that can't bear it and simply die is built into the cost of production.

This last point is important: If you look at the statistics, hundreds of millions of animals a year die before going to slaughter.

Just think about that: Hundreds of millions die before even being shipped to slaughter.

I assume my dilemma at this point is clear. Obviously, I considered myself a good person—an ethical, kind, and thoughtful human being. And yet, here I was, supporting what is clearly a modern-day atrocity. "Our own worst nightmare" is how the *New York Times* describes modern agribusiness, and I was giving this nightmare my money to continue to tail dock, debeak, confine, forcibly impregnate, brand, dehorn, and otherwise brutalize these thinking, feeling creatures.

And the argument that "They're only animals"? Having seen this phrase used to justify slavery and Hitler's "Final Solution," I certainly didn't want to be uttering the phrase "just animals." I read the various justifications for past atrocities—not just from hateful, ignorant people, but from some of America's and Germany's leading citizens: professors, clergy, civic leaders, and politicians. I saw just how easily the vast majority of people went along with the prejudice of their day; how they believed whatever they were taught without question, no matter the contradictions or consequences.

So I couldn't simply accept the line, "They're just animals."

Here is where I should tell you about the great breakthrough, where I went from unquestioningly accepting society's norm to animal advocate. But it didn't happen that way.

I did go vegetarian for a while, late in my first year of college, but soon I convinced myself I was starving on the cafeteria's beans and Cap'n Crunch. To my lasting shame, I went back to eating animals, just like all my friends and family.

But I couldn't stop thinking about what it means to eat meat. Even if they were "just animals," my choices caused them to suffer—suffer terribly and die horribly. My choices deprived them of the life they wanted to live. My choices—the choices I was consciously making, every day—created absolutely unnecessary suffering.

The next year, I was living off campus, entirely responsible for my own food choices. One day, I was looking in the mirror and the thought just came to me: How can I consider myself a good person if I continue to eat animals?

I had no answer.

And then (this is entirely true) the medicine cabinet started shaking, and a deafening *Bam! Bam! Bam!* filled the room.[3]

---

3 It turned out that someone in the adjacent apartment was driving a nail into the other side of the wall. Banal cause, but a fitting punctuation for when my life changed.

I've never eaten another animal.

Now, obviously, there is much more to discuss: everything from nutrition to priorities to optimal advocacy to the future of society.

But before all that are questions that took me so very, very long to fully consider. We each have to ask the questions: What kind of people are we? Will we accept what our society dictates today, or will we write our own story? Will we rationalize the status quo or thoughtfully make our own decisions? Will we oppose cruelty or support slaughter?

Slowly, very slowly, embarrassingly slowly, I came to realize there are more important things in life than accepting the status quo and taking the easiest path. Choosing the road less traveled does not necessitate denial and deprivation. Making our life a part of something real, something larger than ourselves—this expands our life's narrative, enriches our existence, and allows for real meaning and lasting happiness.

History shows that questioning society is necessary in all times. Today, choosing not to eat animals makes a public, powerful, ethical statement—not just about the lives of animals, but about the nature of our character. It shows that we are honestly striving to be truly good, thoughtful people.

FROM Letter to a Young Matt

A Talk in Chicago, Illinois, 2009

One thing long-time vegans often forget is how hard it can be to be vegan in this society. I've forgotten to a large extent, because I'm married to a vegan, have a vegan daughter, and have literally thousands of vegan friends and colleagues.

But if I think back to when I went vegan about two decades ago, I remember some of how hard it was. Not so much finding vegan food (although it was much harder then), but living in a non-vegan world. I had finally come to recognize the brutality that went on behind the scenes, but it seemed no one around me cared. Even worse than that, they mocked and attacked me for being vegan! I mean, not only did they support cruelty, but they ridiculed me for not eating animals!

Of course, I had to show them: how ethical I was, how much cruelty I could purge from my life, how far I would go for the animals. Being vegan became my defining characteristic, and I became obsessed with justifying and glorifying veganism (and, thus, myself). Debates about language, philosophy, and hypotheticals all took on vital importance. I had to take part in any protest that came along: driving long distances, being out in sub-zero weather, getting arrested. I couldn't "turn my back" on the animals. I was just that dedicated!

I'm afraid that if my twenty-one-year-old self met my forty-one-year-old self, prior me would loathe current me. Young Matt would consider Current Matt an intellectual coward, a pathetic sellout, a traitor to veganism. I fear there is nothing I could say to change my mind. I was so self-righteous, so angry, so obsessive.

But, sometimes, I wonder what I *would* say, if I had the chance.

The single most important lesson I've learned in the past twenty years is that the irreducible heart of what matters is suffering. Back then, even though I was absolutely sure I knew everything, I really didn't know anything about suffering. Since then, though, I've developed a chronic disease and experienced times when I thought I was going to die, times when I wished I *would* die. Back then, I worried about abstractions and words and principles; I argued about exploitation, oppression, liberation. I didn't take suffering seriously. Now, knowing what suffering really is, and knowing how much there is in the world, all my previous concerns seem—well, to put it kindly, ridiculous.

I don't know how I could convey this to my younger self, who had never really known suffering. Yet it seems clear to me now that when we make a decision, we should decide based on what leads to the least amount of suffering. This is the bottom line: Something is good and right and ethical if it causes less suffering than the alternatives.

Obviously, Young Matt would crow, "Of course I make ethical choices; that is why I'm a vegan!" But here is what I couldn't understand back then: What I put into my mouth is only a tiny fraction of what is important.

Being surrounded by mocking meat eaters back then, I became obsessed over what I could control: my personal purity. It was only later I came to realize that, despite all my talk about "the animals," I was really only protecting and promoting myself.

It literally took me years to understand that there can be so much more to life than my own purity, my own righteousness. But things that seem painfully obvious to me now—like the fundamental, irreducible importance of suffering—never made it through my anger and self-absorption.

As the saying goes, a smart person learns from his or her own mistakes, but a wise person learns from the mistakes of others. Another error I had to make for myself was the trap of "do something, do anything!" If there was some action going on "for the animals," I had to do it. It never occurred to me to consider exactly what constructive purpose the action served, how much actual good was going to be accomplished, or what the alternative uses of my time and resources might be. I thought only of showing my dedication, of expressing my outrage.

But of course, expressions of outrage aren't going to bring about animal liberation. I finally realized that if I really cared about something more than venting my anger, my actions had to be part of a reasoned, logical strategy. And the plan has to be realistic, not based simply on my desires, my demands of what "must" happen. This strategy has to be grounded in how the world actually is, learning from what history teaches us about how societies change, what psychology and sociology tell us about human nature, and what our capabilities are at the time.

Understanding our capabilities is vital. We don't have infinite resources; we actually have extremely limited time and money, especially compared to the industries that exploit animals. Vegan Outreach's budget isn't even a million dollars a year. It's true that the budget for People for the Ethical Treatment of Animals (PETA) is bigger, and that of The Humane Society of the United States (HSUS) is more than a hundred million dollars annually. But compare these figures to the companies that exploit animals: In 2007, two of these companies—Tyson and Cargill—had revenues of over $115 billion. *Billion*, with a "B"!

After years of unfocused, angry activism, I finally came to realize that if I truly cared about the animals, I had to maximize the amount of good I accomplished with my limited time and resources. And to do so, I had to set aside my ego and stop focusing on what most outraged me personally. Rather, I needed to start from the two fundamental lessons that took me so long to learn:

- Suffering is irreducibly bad. Thus, eliminating suffering is the ultimate good.
- Every time we choose to do one thing, we are choosing not to do another.

I've read a lot and debated a lot, but as much as I've tried I've just not been able to get away from the simple truths:

Eliminating suffering is the ultimate good; and every time we choose to do one thing, we are choosing not to do another.

From these two facts comes Vegan Outreach's first principle, our bottom line and guide: Eliminate as much suffering as possible. Everything we do derives directly from that; we make our choices based on which option will lead to the least amount of suffering.

Of course, there is a lot more to discuss in terms of the hows and whys of optimal advocacy. Bruce Friedrich and I have distilled the lessons of our decades of activism and the insights of hundreds of other activists into our book *The Animal Activist's Handbook.*

Despite all the current horror and suffering, if we take the long view and are willing to devote our limited time and resources to the work that needs to be done, we should be deeply optimistic. If we take suffering seriously and are committed to optimal advocacy, we can each create real, fundamental change, every single day.

Because of the number of individuals suffering and the reason behind this hidden brutality, I believe that animal liberation is the moral imperative of our time. We can be the generation that brings about this next great ethical advance. We should revel—really revel!—in the freedom and opportunity we have, the chance to be a part of something so profound! This is as meaningful and joyous a life as I can imagine.

We have no excuse for waiting. Taking meaningful, concrete action for the animals doesn't require anything other than our choice. You don't need to start a group.

You don't need to pass a law. You just have to make the simple but profound and life-changing choice to be a part of this vital work.

In the end, in our hearts, we know that regardless of what we think of ourselves, our actions reveal the kind of person we really are. We can each make the choice, right here, right now, to join together and dedicate our lives to a larger purpose, to maximize the amount of good we accomplish, to really change the world for the better.

Is Vegan Outreach Right about How Many Animals Suffer to Death?

Harish Sethu

This piece originally appeared on Counting Animals'
Web site October, 2011

There is no dispute over the fact that an over-whelming majority of the animals that die at the hands of humans are killed for food. But, unfortunately, it is also true that they receive a smaller share of human compassion than that warranted by either their numbers or the intensity of their suffering. Few organizations have tried to expand this share as unceasingly and single-mindedly as Vegan Outreach, a small non-profit focused on reducing animal suffering. However, in presenting its argument and explaining why it exists, Vegan Outreach makes a startling claim about animals used for food:

> [E]very year, hundreds of millions of animals—many times more than the number killed for fur, in shelters,

and in laboratories combined—don't even make it to slaughter. They actually suffer to death.

Just to make sure nobody missed what is startling here, let me emphasize that Vegan Outreach is not comparing the number killed for food against the number killed for other mentioned reasons; it is comparing the number who suffer to death in the food industry even before they reach the moment of slaughter against the total number killed for all of those other reasons combined. Is Vegan Outreach right, or is this claim just a well-meaning hyperbole? Well, let's examine this claim step by step for the United States, starting with the animals killed in shelters, for fur, and in laboratories.

ANIMALS KILLED IN SHELTERS, FOR FUR, AND IN LABORATORIES

In shelters: There are thousands of independent community shelters in the United States that are not monitored by any national organization. Some states, such as California, require shelters to report euthanasia statistics, but most states do not. Estimates of the number of companion animals killed in shelters in the United States are usually based on extrapolation from the data for states such as California or some other sample of shelters for which data is available. The HSUS estimates[1] that the

---

1 "Common Questions about Animal Shelters," The Humane Society of the United States, May 3, 2013: www.humanesociety.org/animal_community/resources/qa/common_questions_on_shelters.html.

number of companion animals killed in shelters in the United States today is around four million each year.

For fur: The overwhelming majority of the animals we kill for fur in the United States are either wild animals that are trapped or ranch-raised mink from fur farms. In the most recent year for which data is available (2011) from the National Furbearer Harvest Database,[2] we trapped and killed about 6,764,370 wild animals. According to a US Department of Agriculture (USDA) report on mink pelts,[3] the number of mink killed in fur farms in 2011 was about 3,091,470. That makes a total of about 9,855,840 animals killed for fur annually.

In laboratories: The most recent USDA publication on animal use in research[4] reports that 1,134,693 animals covered by the Animal Welfare Act were used in research in 2010. There is no publicly available data on animals not covered by the Animal Welfare Act. However, the Department of Defense (DOD), which reports on all animals it uses in research, offers us a clue. Its most recent report on animal care and use[5] suggests that 90.26 percent of the animals used in research in fiscal year 2007 were those

2 "U.S. Fur Harvest 1970–present Statistics by State, Region and Nation" via National Furbearer Harvest Statistics Database, Association of Fish & Wildlife Agencies: http://fishwildlife.org/?section=furbearer_management_resources.

3 "Mink," USDA, July 6, 2012: http://usda01.library.cornell.edu/usda/current/Mink/Mink-07-06-2012.pdf.

4 *Annual Report: Animal Usage by Fiscal Year (2010)* USDA, Animal and Plant Health Inspection Service, July 2011.

5 *Animal Care and Use Programs for Fiscal Years 2006 and 2007*, Department of Defense.

not covered by the Animal Welfare Act (rats, mice, birds, and most non-mammals). If we assume that DOD labs are representative of other labs that use animals, we are led to an estimate of the number of animals used in research each year at approximately 11,646,000.

ANIMALS WHO SUFFER TO DEATH

Caged layer hens: In both intensity and duration, the suffering experienced by layer hens in conventional battery cages has no parallel. Extreme confinement with prolonged suppression of natural instincts leads to frustration, anxiety, and aggression. Constant pecking by other hens and abrasion with wire-mesh cages cause an eventual loss of feathers and bald patches of exposed skin. Continued pecking on the featherless skin contributes to what the industry calls "tissue pecking," which may lead to death. I am not sure there is a worse way to die, but according to F. Bailey Norwood and Jayson L. Lusk, professors of agricultural economics and authors of *Compassion, by the Pound: The Economics of Farm Animal Welfare*, one-third of layer hen mortality can be attributed to this. But again, every hen who dies in her cage is one who suffers to death, whether she dies of tissue pecking, cage layer fatigue (an extreme form of osteoporosis), egg peritonitis, or starvation as a result of having gotten herself stuck in the cage wires with no way to reach food and water.

In counting hens who suffer to death, I will only consider those hens who die during the laying period in a conventional cage (and not during the rearing period before they begin to lay eggs), a distinction that is only rarely made in both academic and industry estimates of the mortality rate. According to a recent study, published in *Poultry Science* in 2009,[6] the mortality rate during the laying period of hens in conventional cages ranges from 7.78 percent to 15.8 percent depending on the strain. To be conservative, I will use the lowest number, 7.78 percent, in this article. According to the most recent USDA report on chickens and eggs,[7] the number of egg laying hens totaled 351 million in the United States (which includes about 296 million hens whose eggs we eat and about 52 million hens whose eggs are used to hatch new chickens we eat). Since a hen lays eggs for about two years, about 351 divided by two, or 175.5 million hens begin laying eggs during each year. According to the United Egg Producers,[8] as of March 2012, production from caged systems is about 94.3 percent of the total. With that, we can estimate that about 12,876,000 hens actually suffer to death annually.

Chickens Dead on Arrival

Yes, the industry uses the term "dead on arrival" for animals that expire between the time they are put into crates/trucks for transportation to the slaughterhouse

---

6 R. Singh et al., "Production Performance and Egg Quality of Four Strains of Laying Hens Kept in Conventional Cages and Floor Pens," *Poultry Science* 88(2), February 2009.

7 "Chickens and Eggs," USDA, December 23, 2013: http://usda 01.library.cornell.edu/usda/nass/ChicEggs//2010s/2013/ChicE-ggs-12-23-2013.pdf.

8 "General US Stats: Egg Industry Fact Sheet," United Egg Producers, Revised June 2012: http://www.unitedegg.org/GeneralStats/default. cfm.

and the scheduled moment of slaughter. Chickens arrive dead for a number of reasons, including dislocated or broken hips from rough handling, congestive heart failure from the stress of catching and transport, exposure to cold or excessive heat, or just from starvation because of feed withdrawn from them in their last days to reduce fecal contamination. These are all animals who suffer to death even before they reach slaughter. Agri Stats, Inc., a statistical research and analysis firm serving agribusiness companies, is quoted in a 2005 article in the *Journal of Applied Poultry Research*[9] as having estimated the percentage of broiler chickens who are dead on arrival at 0.35 percent in the United States. According to the USDA report on poultry slaughter,[10] 8,428,814,000 chickens were turned into meat in 2012, and so it can be estimated that about 29,604,000 broiler chickens died during transportation for slaughter. The pre-slaughter mortality rate is even higher for spent hens who, having been confined in a cage for most of their lives, have more fragile bones. Data from another study[11] conducted in Italy (its dead-on-arrival numbers

---

9 C. W. Ritz, A. B. Webster, and M. Czarick III. "Evaluation of Hot Weather Thermal Environment and Incidence of Mortality Associated with Broiler Live Haul." *Journal of Applied Poultry Research* 14 (3), 2005.

10 "Poultry Slaughter," National Agricultural Statistics Service, Agricultural Statistics Board, USDA, January 24, 2013: http:// usda01.library.cornell.edu/usda/nass/PoulSlau//2010s/2013/Poul-Slau-01-24-2013.txt.

11 M. Petracci et al. "Preslaughter Mortality in Broiler Chickens, Turkeys, and Spent Hens Under Commercial Slaughtering." *Poultry Science* 85 (9), September 2006.

for broiler chickens match the US numbers and, there-fore, it is a fair assumption to extrapolate to the case of spent hens in the United States) suggests that the dead-on-arrival rate for spent hens is as high as 1.22 percent. According to another USDA report on poultry production and value,[12] 178,313,000 hens were sold for slaughter in 2012 and so about 2,175,000 layer hens suffered to death on their way to slaughter. That's a total of about 31,780,000 chickens who suffer to death annually during transport before they even reach the moment of slaughter!

Broiler Chickens with Leg Deformities

An all-consuming focus on weight gain and feed con-version efficiencies have led to increasing percentages of chickens in the broiler industry with legs that can-not adequately support their weight. Severely lame birds cannot walk or even stand. They can starve to death if they are unable to reach food and water. They die a pain-ful death from a variety of consequences of leg defor-mities including limb torsion, ruptured tendons, swollen foot pads, and severe lesions, ulcers, or hemorrhages. In the scientific literature on poultry health (such as in this article[13] in *Poultry Science*), among the most frequently quoted studies on leg deformities in broiler chickens is a

---

12 National Agricultural Statistics Service, USDA, "Poultry Produc-tion and Value," April 2013.

13 C. P. Laster et al. "Effects of Dietary Roxarsone Supplementation, Lighting Program, and Season on the Incidence of Leg Abnormalities in Broiler Chickens." *Poultry Science* 78 (2), February 1999.

national survey that found that broiler flocks experience 1.1 percent mortality due to leg abnormalities. According to the National Chicken Council,[14] mortality rate of broilers these days is 3.8 percent, but I will consider only the 1.1 percent who die of leg problems as having suffered to death. Since 8,428,814,000 chickens in 2012 survived the 3.8 percent mortality rate to get processed into meat for human consumption, we can estimate that the 1.1 percent who suffered to death number about 96,379,000.

SO, IS VEGAN OUTREACH RIGHT?

Now, let's total these numbers and visualize their magnitudes below to see where we stand:

- Estimated number of animals killed for fur, in shelters, and in laboratories combined: **25,502,000**
- Estimated number of chickens who suffer to death without even making it to slaughter: **141,035,000**

These are the numbers (with conservative estimates culled from industry reports and scientific journals), and we have not even covered all the other ways by which millions of chickens can slowly suffer to death (such as from respiratory diseases caused by exposure to elevated

---

14 National Chicken Council. *US Broiler Performance*, 2011.

levels of noxious ammonia). And we did not even start counting the turkeys, pigs, cows, and, yes, billions of fish! But we don't have to. The answer to the question posed in the title of this post is already evident.

Vegan Outreach, sadly for the suffering animals, is spectacularly right.

Real Courage (or: Learning from Past Mistakes)

Animal Rights National Conference 2013, Washington, DC

Meat eaters love to change the subject and complain about vegans' sense of smug superiority. But I can say it is very likely that I truly am superior to most of you: I have made more mistakes.

I stopped eating animals back in the 1980s. In the years after that, I made an absurd number of mistakes. Probably the main reason I wanted to publish *The Animal Activist's Handbook* is to try to help others avoid at least some of the mistakes I made.

One of my biggest mistakes was lacking courage, but perhaps not in the way you think.

Over the years, people advised me to say I was vegan for my health. "That way," I was told, "people won't be threatened by you. Everyone cares about their health, so they won't feel judged."

Of course, I didn't go along with that. I protested, "But I'm vegan for so many reasons! The animals! The Earth! Human health!" Back then, our attitude was to "win an argument with a meat eater" (the title of a famous poster of the time). The approach was to try to overwhelm a meat eater with an endless list of what we believed were "facts," which simplified to the following: All ills in the world, from impotence to hunger to ozone depletion to serial killings, were all because of meat.

Do you see the problem? It was all about me: why *I* was vegan, how I was so right, how I wanted to win an argument, because meat eaters were so very wrong, wrong, wrong!

Now, in sympathy with Young Matt and the rest of us back then, there really was no other example. We all spouted endless claims of water usage and declining fertility. No matter how absurd a claim, if something sounded even vaguely anti-meat or pro-vegetables, we parroted it like the indoctrinated missionaries we were.

On a basic human level, this is understandable. We were a tiny minority, surrounded by meat eaters—meat eaters who often mocked us. You can see why we were so eager, so desperate to justify ourselves, to strike back, to try to belittle those who belittled us, to win.

Of course, looking at it rationally today, we know any discomfort we experience is nothing compared to what farmed animals endure. But this perspective would have required me to think beyond myself and my self-interest.

I regret my lack of courage, my inability to get past my need to justify myself, praise veganism, and blame meat eaters for every ill.

Of course, if you had pointed this out to me back then, I would have been outraged: "I am courageous! Do you know how hard it is to be vegan in the world? Look at this sheet of 'facts': Meat eating is terrible! Veganism is the only way!"

Indeed, twenty-five years ago I would have joined the many people who attack Vegan Outreach. VO has been called "pro-vivisection," because we point out that we each have limited time and resources and thus should focus our advocacy where we can have the biggest impact. We've been called "pro-egg," because we believe honesty best serves the animals, and thus point out all studies related to diet and disease, not just cherry-picked ones that seem to support veganism. We've been condemned as "anti-vegan," because we admit that not every animal product causes the same amount of suffering. And we're called "anti-human," because, for example, we don't loudly claim milk "causes" Crohn's disease (this one is especially ironic, given that I developed Crohn's disease years after going vegan). Finally, Vegan Outreach is hated and attacked for ignoring philosophy and intra-vegan debates, and, especially, for not promoting only pure, absolutist veganism.

Twenty-five years ago I would have been disgusted by Vegan Outreach: "How can they sleep at night?!" I assume you're smarter than I was, and again see the flaw: This is *still* all about me, my veganism, my philosophy, my "consistency," my demands. "What do we want? Animal Rights! When do we want it? *Now!*"

My interactions with meat eaters consisted of preaching an endless stream of horrors: "You are causing all this! You need to be *just . . . like . . . me!*" It was so important to chant, to insist, to pursue purity—much more important than working constructively to bring about actual change.

I only realized later that the truly courageous path is to set aside anything about me and see what can be done to reduce the amount of real suffering in the world. Real courage requires working to lessen suffering as much as possible as quickly as possible, regardless of what we want, what sounds good to us, what seems to justify our current lifestyle.

Don't get me wrong! I'm not saying that being vegan isn't good or important. But however important our personal, day-to-day choices are, choosing effective advocacy for the animals is far, far more important. However much good we accomplish by being vegan every day of the rest of our entire lives . . . well, we can do more good than that in just an hour of honest, psychologically sound activism—or in just a minute, by donating to effective advocacy.

To really accomplish good in the world, we can't be like Young Matt. We can't focus on what sounds good to us. We can't just rattle off facts that we find compelling, repeat anything that seems to justify our veganism, latch on to the latest "study" that "proves" what we want to believe.

And we can't just "do something, do anything." Instead, we have to look at the overall, real-world impact of our advocacy, and compare those consequences to other alternatives we could pursue with our limited time and resources.

This isn't easy, in part because it is often quite outside

the norm of advocacy. It is just so easy to fall into the trap of thinking, "People are selfish, I'll appeal to self-interest!" Or taking anecdotes as data, such as "Marcie went vegan for reason X, so everyone must promote X!" Effective advocates look beyond what we think or what motivates us and those around us. We need to put aside what makes veganism sound good to us and focus on what will move non-vegetarians to take steps that actually reduce suffering.

For example, we can't focus on something that seems noncontroversial, something that seems to appeal to everyone, if doing so might encourage someone to stop eating big animals and instead eat more birds and fishes; anyone who just gives up red meat causes much, much more suffering.

In other words, we must consider all the actual consequences of our advocacy.

I don't mean to preach. I wasted so many opportunities, turned off so many people, because I was all about: "Don't you see this list of 'facts'? Vegan first! Vegan only!" It took me years—and the help of truly courageous people—before I could set aside my insecurities and ego and personal needs, and focus instead on practical, realistic advocacy that actually helps animals.

Yet I don't know what I could have said to Young Matt. I was so angry, so filled with the odd combination of insecurity masked by self-righteousness. It sounded so compelling back then: We had to document how every problem in the universe came from our exploitation of animals! We had to defend the integrity of veganism! We had to be pure and consistent in our insistence on everything we wanted right now!

Veganism! Abolition! No compromise!

It is an intoxicating siren song.

But let me leave you with a few decades of data: Since I came to the first March for the Animals in 1990, Jack, Anne, and I have met hundreds of vegans who burned with an absolutist flame. Many loudly attacked Vegan Outreach as pathetic sellouts, gutless compromisers, collaborating capitalists, and welfarists.

Basically none of them are around today. There are, of course, new adherents, new Young Matts. But if you look, you'll actually see a number of truly courageous people, people who have put aside their ego and are focused on helping the animals as much as possible, every day.[1]

And if you remember only one actual fact, remember this: In 2013, the number of animals slaughtered in the United States is declining.

For decades, people gave up red meat for self-centered health and environmental reasons, and this led to a vast increase in the number of chickens and fishes butchered every year. But now, since 2006, the number of animals suffering and dying in the United States has been going down. Interestingly—to me at least—2006 was also the first year Vegan Outreach distributed more than a million booklets.

---

1 For a list of Adopt a College leafleters, see www.adoptacollege.org/stats.php. Profiles of Vegan Outreach's top leafleters can be found at www.veganoutreach.org/enewsletter/profiles.html.

I hope you have more courage than I did, and will join with those who go beyond self-interest, who put aside the pursuit of philosophy and personal purity. Instead, we can do the real, concrete work: day-to-day, person-to-person outreach that is actually helping animals, literally changing the world.

An Open Mind

Interview with EarthSave Portland, 2003

What were some of your first activist experiences, and how have they influenced the activist you are today?

My first experiences were with the local Animal Rights Community (ARC) of Greater Cincinnati's campaign against Procter & Gamble (run, in part, by the group In Defense of Animals)—including getting arrested at the shareholders' meeting. We also did anti-fur demonstrations. Jack Norris (then special events coordinator of ARC) realized that a few protests a season weren't going to change anyone's behavior, so in the winter of 1990–91, he, Phil Murray (now of Pangea[1]), and I took a "Make This Year Fur-Free" banner and anti-fur leaflets to cultural events. We held dozens and dozens of "protests" that cold winter—nine in one weekend alone.

I think these events tended to show Jack, Phil, and me that the "standard" activism was neither sustainable nor going to bring about significant change. (Joe Espi-

---

1 See www.veganstore.com.

nosa had a similar experience,[2] as I'm sure have many others.) I think that, between the three of us, Jack, Phil, and I had the right combination of anger and dedication (to keep us going in the face of relative failure) and open minds (to keep us searching for new ideas). Anne [Green, vice president of Vegan Outreach in 2003] added a lot to the evolution of ideas from 1992 on.

Why Why Vegan? *What made the three of you get together and say "Hey, a pamphlet!"? What made you choose to found VO on the principle of direct outreach?*

We never really had an "epiphany" like that. We were— and still are—always searching, debating, trying, listening, and evolving.

The evolution is apparent in the Vegan Outreach literature. You can just look at the very first one-page booklet (*Vegetarianism*) that Jack did (funded mostly by Phil's last National Merit Scholarship check) in 1990, how it changed to *And Justice for All*, to *Vegan Outreach* (all copies of which we collated, stapled, and folded by hand) to the many versions of *Why Vegan?* and the [then] upcoming *Try Vegetarian!* But just looking at the change in that piece of literature fails to mention the *Vegan Starter Pack*, the Vegan Advocacy booklet (and other materials we provide, such as the Christian Vegetarian Association's *What Would Jesus Eat . . . Today?*, PETA's Alec Baldwin–version of the video *Meet Your Meat*),

---

2 Joe Espinosa & Marsha Forsman, "Why Vegan Outreach?" Vegan Outreach, spring 2003: www.veganoutreach.org/advocacy/whyvo.html.

as well as Jack's leafleting college campuses across the country for two years, and subsequent events.

Toss in our fur campaign, getting arrested, holding "Stop Eating Animals" banners on bridges and street corners, fasting in public, dressing up like pigs. There was no straight progression to what we do now, and we will continue to explore new things, and adopt and/or endorse those we find efficacious.

So, in short, we are where we are because of the following reasons:

1. We are and have been dedicated to maximizing our impact on the amount of suffering.
2. We're willing to try new things.
3. We're not afraid to admit failure.

Many veg groups focus on the health benefits of a veg diet because they think it's most effective to cater to people's self-interest. VO has repeatedly stressed that the key focus is reducing animal suffering. Why did you choose this avenue?

As often presented by vegans, the "health argument" is exaggerated at best, but often factually incorrect. It is amazing the contortions some advocates will go through to try to vilify any and all animal products as "deadly poison," and it's not surprising that the public sees through this propaganda.

Given that nearly everyone wants to continue to consume animal products, they seize upon any reason to ignore the vegetarian message. When the veg advocate's message is counter to everything else the public has been told (chicken and fish are healthful, low-fat dairy is a good source of calcium), or the latest diet fad (the Zone, Atkins, Eat Right for Your Type), they aren't going to heed the seemingly restrictive and alien pronouncements of vegans. (Here's a mental exercise that might be useful: Try to put yourself into the mind-set of a "normal" middle-class American, and then imagine how you would react to a raw-food advocate saying all cooked food is poison.)

Perhaps more importantly, the health argument has contributed to the increase in the number of chickens and fish killed and consumed in this country. Without getting into questions of relative sentience, this horrifying rise in the number of animals killed for food can't be seen as a good thing. Since, as you point out, most groups avoid the issue of cruelty, they cannot logically reject this approach. At the very least, this increase in animals killed should lead most advocacy groups to reevaluate their approach.

Fundamentally, Vegan Outreach believes that promoting selfishness is not the best way to reduce suffering. Recognition of and concern for others is the key; a basic rejection of cruelty is what we seek. Most people know that the standard American diet is not our healthiest habit, but most people don't know that the standard American farm is "our worst nightmare."

You advocate a positive, nonconfrontational approach to animal liberation that eschews demonstrations and other similar types of activism. In a recent interview, you said, "More people are realizing that we aren't going to chant and scream animal liberation into existence." How did this philosophy of offering humble, honest information as a primary activist strategy develop for you?

Trial and error, and plenty of bashing my head against a brick wall. I wish I could say that I had a brilliant insight into the human psyche from day one, but that isn't true. For years, I acted from the anger and near-misanthropy that many activists have.

This fury—understandable and justified—is certainly real, and a start for many. But fundamentally, it isn't about my anger (or ego or needs). It is about those suffering. It is about creating the greatest change we can.

In general, people (read: our target audience, the ones who currently support modern animal agriculture) don't want to be miserable. They want to be happy. Only those who seek solace (and/or identity) in rage will react well to arrogance and loathing; we can't limit our advocacy only to the conceited.

A lot of new animal activists operate out of anger and despair. In fact, a lot of activists spend much of their lives depressed, angry, and burned out. What sparked your transition to a life of joy and openness, of becoming "an example of a life that others would admire and be interested in understanding"?

Again, I wish that I could give an answer that would be inspiring to all readers, but my personal views are a result of odd bounces and lucky twists. If I had gone to Georgia Tech instead of the University of Cincinnati, if I had ended up on the engineers' floor of the dorm instead of with a vegetarian roommate. . . It's all the butterfly effect, although some elements (like meeting Jack, of course) are obviously central. But for me, Anne [Green] has been, far and away, the key to everything.

Here are two seemingly at-odds facts:

A. As mentioned, fury and/or despair are entirely understandable. I think most people deny/block out the reality of all the suffering in the world—a psychological defense mechanism. Those who don't suppress this truth yet don't feel anger and/or hopelessness are often psychopaths.

B. Perhaps the best way to have a significant impact on the state of the world is to find a better space in life, to be an example of a desirable, meaningful life.

Getting from A to B is vital for the animals, but an incredibly difficult path. This should, I think, be a priority for everyone who cares about reducing and preventing suffering.

What has most surprised you during all your VO experiences?

That I didn't die of stomach ulcers from worrying about upcoming leafleting and public speaking. Those activities used to make me sick with worry for days beforehand. I now have Crohn's disease, though, so . . .

What's been your most difficult/challenging speaking experience?

One was certainly the first time I led a Students for Animal Rights (SAR) meeting at the University of Illinois. I had fought against taking over the group, but it was either that or having the group fold. I was terrified before the first meeting, wrote draft after draft of my opening speech, read it to Phil, and read it to Jack over the phone. I then read it right from the paper to a classroom full of potential members. Only one was still with SAR a month later, but that person was Anne, so I guess it was ultimately a success!

Before the AR2003 East conference, I was the featured speaker for the day at a regional 4-H camp. Many (if not most) of the people were hostile and had a caricatured view of animal rights going in: i.e., that vegans consider animals to be more important than people, that animal rights activists engage in "terrorism" and violence against animal industries, that we hated farmers. It would have been easy to present only areas foreign to them (the health/"deadly poison" argument, religious veganism, absolute animal rights, rejection of all animal "exploitation"—e.g., bees for honey, cats and dogs as "pets"), but not only would that have accomplished less than nothing, those concepts aren't what is truly important.

Finding common ground is key and shouldn't be hard. Most of the people in that, or any, audience reject cruelty and can identify with my underlying message: an opposition to causing suffering. These high-school students, many of whom had grown up on small farms, also had reason to reject the corporatization of animal agriculture. Not just the cruelty involved, but that they had all seen friends and relatives put out of business.

We expect others to open their minds to our message, to reject their history and habits—everything they've been taught in the past. We can't really expect this of others unless we also have an open mind, one that allows us to see the point of view of others and their motivations.

Jack Norris has branched off on his own with Making Sense of Nutrition Research. *How has that affected VO's effectiveness and direction?*

As I hope is clear, Vegan Outreach has always been seeking to find the best way to reduce suffering. One thing we have found in all our time doing outreach—especially in Jack's two years of leafleting across the country, when he met tens of thousands of people—is that there are many, many failed vegetarians. For some advocates, this is a foreign concept ("Veganism is the ultimate diet! It is the only path to real health!"), and most advocacy organizations are dedicated to advancing the standard vegan party line (presenting animal products as "deadly poison," and veganism as inherently perfect).

(Again, see the parallel with raw foodists, where any ill health is your body "purging," and anyone who quits was just "addicted" to cooked foods and not dedicated enough.)

Few individuals or organizations are really committed to an honest, candid analysis of nutrition as it applies to vegetarian diets (especially veganism), and the string of failed vegetarians (including many celebrities, such as Michael Stipe of REM, Tracy "Mrs. Michael J. Fox" Pollan, Madonna, Drew Barrymore, and others) that has been the result.

If we want to prevent suffering, we have to work hard to guarantee that everyone can stay a healthy vegan. For this reason, Jack's focus on nutrition is in keeping with Vegan Outreach's general mission. However, there is also a practical concern: being able to pay the rent and put food on the table. I've been in a fortunate position with Anne teaching at Carnegie Mellon University. But Jack has, for all intents and purposes, been a full-time activist for more than a decade, without means to make a reasonable living.

How has VO changed since its inception?

We're always changing (as discussed above), trying to find the best ways to prevent suffering.

One thing that I think has remained the same, though (and it is relatively unique to Vegan Outreach) is the amount of, shall we say, "personality" the group has. We don't claim to have all the answers. We're just three folks trying to do our best and help others do their best, with what knowledge we've accumulated and the resources we have at the time. We disagree among ourselves (vehemently at times), make mistakes and enemies (e.g., "You have become a corrupt marketing arm of the meat and dairy industries"), but we keep plugging away.

Karen Dawn of DawnWatch.com recently asked

how we would describe Vegan Outreach. "Fanatically anti-dogmatic" is a good start. Being able to promote values such as humility, joy, and humor is another upside to our more personal approach.

What are the biggest challenges VO faces now?

Raising money.

It is hard, with all the cruelty, abuse, and suffering going on in the world right now to donate to something as abstract as promoting veganism. Human nature responds to the known and immediate. Donors react to the picture and story of an individual animal, with a specific plea, rather than a nebulous "Help us print *Try Vegetarian!*, and somewhere people will stop eating animals, and down the road some animals won't be bred and suffer in factory farms." (This is, of course, true for me as well. There are two cats I know that are headed to the shelter for lack of a home. Anne has developed a terrible allergy since our daughter Ellen was born, or we would take them. The plight of these cats has caused me a great deal of grief, although it is nothing compared to the suffering going on in factory farms and industrial slaughterhouses.)

It is also very hard to get people to fund honest and balanced nutritional research and reporting as well.

To generalize, people like to back an immediate winner, someone who has the sure-sounding, inspiring, attention-grabbing message. And this doesn't even begin to comment on the state of today's economy, especially as it relates to our standard member—a college student.

Vegan Outreach has existed for years on an annual

budget that is less than what some groups put toward relatively minor projects. We've distributed millions of copies of *Why Vegan?* and *Vegetarian Living!* as a tiny, relatively unknown group. Yet so much more could be done; e.g., having copies of *Why Vegan?* and *Try Vegetarian!* on display in every willing health-food store, library, bookstore, coffeehouse, and restaurant—not to mention having activists regularly leafleting their local high school and college—would reach so many interested people for a relative pittance.

What do you hope VO will look like five to ten years from now?

"Hope" is a lot different than "expect." As the saying goes, "Wish for the best, and plan for the worst."

But I generally don't think about the future of Vegan Outreach, knowing how much has changed in the past. We may well discover something else that proves more effective at preventing suffering, or maybe a new source of support (and/or inspiration) may come forward.

PERSONAL QUESTIONS
2003

Who's the head chef in the family—you or Anne? What's your specialty?

I make the bread that Anne earns. She also does cleanup— she loves creating order from chaos! While I am, at heart, a meat-and-potatoes guy, we prefer ethnic food—Mexican, Thai, and Indian, mostly. We use a lot of Gimme Lean (order cases at the co-op and freeze it) and Tofurky slices (ditto). I also make good seitan dishes.

Why did you study engineering and public policy (EPP) in grad school?

As I finished up my degree in aerospace engineering, I wanted to do something useful, but also use my engineering background. I won a Department of Energy Global Change Fellowship to work on global warming/climate change and related fields. I started in environmental engineering at the University of Illinois, got booted from that program, and moved down to the Department of Forest Ecology, where I took an MS.

After Anne got a job at Carnegie Mellon, my fellowship transferred to engineering and public policy there. I lasted a wee bit longer at that program, so I was able to take an MS when booted, moved to environmental engineering, worked at the Department of Biology at the University of Pittsburgh, and eventually "retired" from the academic world to do Vegan Outreach full time.

What books are you reading now?

I tend to listen to books on tape (when I'm driving, cooking, stuffing envelopes), as I don't have time to read. Oddly enough, right now I'm listening to *That Old Ace in the Hole* by E. Annie Proulx (author of *The Shipping*

News). Its underlying point is to expose corporate hog farms, and it makes a darn good case against them.

Before that, I listened to *Harry Potter and the Order of the Phoenix.* The same reader [Jim Dale] does all five books, and he's tremendous. You really feel like you know the characters—the voices he gives them, the inflections, the emotions, etc. The book is a heartbreaking study of human frailties and failures; far more moving and insightful than most other fiction I've encountered.

I finished listening to it driving back from AR2003 East, and almost cried. Within ten days of its release, Anne and I had finished listening to it, and Ellen had read it. It was so intense that Ellen isn't inclined to read it again right away. She has read all the others multiple times; the third (*Harry Potter and the Prisoner of Azkaban*) over twenty times.

And before that, I listened to Margaret Atwood's *Oryx and Crake.* In it, "humanity" goes vegan, in a fashion.

Favorite cookbook?

None. I tend to stick with what I've done and sometimes try new ideas I have. My last favorite cookbook was *Vegan Vittles* [by Jo Stepaniak].

Favorite hobbies?

My priority when I have time is to spend it with Anne and Ellen.

I like to cook, garden, read, and take pictures. I would like to really take up golf, because that would force me to take time out from work and be outside. I watch a lot of golf while stuffing envelopes (I got a "Best Dad" award, with the clarification "even though he watches a lot of golf.")

Eating and beer are also way up there, too.

Favorite magazine?

Wired. Optimism and fun. Before they became mindlessly pro-[President George] Bush, *The Economist* (e.g., "What Humans Owe to Animals")[3] was the "best" magazine in the world.

What is the first thing you think of when you wake up in the morning?

Anne and Ellen do a "puppet" show (using Ellen's Beanie Babies) called "15 Minutes with Cats." Once, they had the dad cat wake up and the first thing he said was, "Huh, uh, where's my computer?!"

What is most important in life?

Being with Anne, which for me is key to being as happy as possible. I think that living an ethical life

---

3 The article was published in the magazine on August 19, 1995.

can provide meaning, purpose, and the possibility of accomplishment for life, which I think can be central to happiness.

Favorite foods?

Ethiopian, mostly because I can't make it myself. Specifically, Meskerem in Washington, DC, for which I'm eternally grateful to Scott Williams, formerly of FARM. Good Thai food is right up there, and Vegetable Garden outside of DC is wonderful. The lettuce wraps at P.F. Chang's are right up there, and actual New Mexican in New Mexico is a three-times-a-day treat. Boxes of expired but still edible vegan donuts are always welcome! St. Pauli Girl is currently my favorite beer.

Chocolate or vanilla?

Chocolate mint.

What model was your first car?

Buick station wagon, with a rusted out floor and a huge, 120-mph-capable engine. Not that I would know about the latter.

Favorite movie?

The Big Chill. I think *Out of Africa* is the best "big screen" movie.

Who are your role models?

Growing up, I greatly admired Carl Sagan, Ansel Adams, and Henry David Thoreau.

Dream vacation?

Visiting the McDonald's-funded Vegan Outreach office in New Zealand, where other people stuff envelopes and answer the phone!

"Life Is Good!"

A 2013 Interview with a College Student

What does it mean to "want a vegan world, not a vegan club"?

We have limited time and resources. We can spend it worrying about ingredient lists, arguing philosophy, praising veganism, and enforcing definitions/excluding people from being "vegan." Or we can work to help those whose choices currently hurt animals, and help them start making choices to reduce the number of animals bred into factory farms and butchered in industrial slaughterhouses. In other words, we can focus on promoting our personal veganism, or we can get new people to start taking steps that help animals.

How long have you considered yourself vegan? How has your attitude toward vegans, as a group, evolved over that timeframe?

I stopped eating animals sometime in the Stone Age—back in the 1980s—and evolved to veganism a few years after that. At that time, I was a total vegan clubber, worried about justifying and praising my veganism/attacking and "winning arguments" with meat eaters. I would repeat anything and everything I heard that sounded vaguely pro-vegan or anti-meat, regardless of its veracity or its actual impact on others.

It took me years to realize that how I felt about veganism or the issues that seemed (to me) to be related to veganism were ultimately irrelevant. The animals mattered. Period. And if I wanted to help as many animals as possible—to reduce as much suffering as possible—my actions had to be focused on the animals, not me or veganism.

Psychologists have a good idea why and how people change, and it isn't by being confronted by an egotistical absolutist who cares only about his or her definition of veganism. People change when they open their hearts and minds to change. We can help bring this about by reaching them where they are and focusing on the first step they can take, instead of glorifying and demanding the last step we took.

Why did you initially embrace veganism?

When I was a freshman in college, my roommate was a vegetarian. He told me about the cruelty of modern agribusiness. I didn't change at first, and there was a false start, but I eventually stopped eating animals. This evolved over time—I gave up factory-farmed eggs, and started buying "free-range" from the local health-food store. I bought only Amish cheese. And then I gave it all up. I finally got to the point where habit and convenience didn't outweigh wanting to make choices that caused animals to be killed.

Why do you currently embrace veganism?

I actually wouldn't say I "embrace" veganism. For the reasons I discuss in "A Meaningful Life" [see appendix] my goal in life is to reduce as much suffering in the world as possible. But my personal food choices are only a small part of that. Being a good, joyous example; writing constructive booklets and essays; doing and promoting effective and efficient outreach; living simply so more money can go to the animals—that is what I seek to embrace.

How did you perceive veganism as a lifestyle before you were vegan?

Hard! Bordering on crazy and impossible!

How do you perceive veganism as a lifestyle now?

I know many vegans like to say, "Veganism isn't a diet; it is a lifestyle!" They then go on to say, "And the lifestyle includes X, Y, and Z," and X, Y, and Z just happen to align with their personal views: their politics, their other habits, their philosophy.

Not surprisingly, I was like that, too. It took me a long time to realize this was, at best, a waste of our limited resources. But worse than that, this attitude just serves to put up barriers to others. A new person is much less likely to consider taking any step when we insist on taking the last step first, especially if that last step requires many things other than what we eat.

Now, I only care about more people learning the hidden cruelties of modern agribusiness. This is how more people can take the first step toward helping these animals. Reading and/or worrying about debates about veganism . . . well, this isn't an efficient use of limited resources.

What was your attitude toward food before you were vegan?

I would guess I had a pretty typical midwestern attitude toward food. I really didn't like vegetables (except corn on the cob), and steak was a much-anticipated "special treat" food. I was a middle-class kid who dreamed of a good career, a bigger house, a fast car, a fancy stereo system, trips, and good food.

What is your attitude toward food now, as a vegan?

We have such great, amazingly tasty food today. I look forward to meals—choosing is difficult! It is much different than when I first went vegan, I can't begin to tell you. Between being poor and the lack of options, it was rough. For a while in Cincinnati, there was a little place—Take Outrageous—that had this amazing deep-fried tofu sandwich with a sauce we thought was infused with some addictive drug. We would each have one and were absolutely tormented because we couldn't afford another. Now, I eat things at least that good nearly every day, and I don't have to fret about affording my next meal. Life is good!

Do you feel camaraderie toward others who identify as vegan? Why or why not?

I tend to feel the deepest connection to fellow utilitarians dedicated to practical, efficient, and effective work to reduce suffering.

A Personal Note Regarding Choices and Suffering

Why Vegan Outreach Blog, March, 2013

Recently, our good friend Brian posted an excerpt from "Letter to a Young Matt" on Facebook, and there was a bit of pushback from a few quarters, specifically to this portion:

> Of course, if these billions of [food] animals lived happy, healthy lives and had quick, painless deaths, then our goal of reducing as much suffering as possible would lead us [to work] elsewhere.

This seems to have been taken by some as a tacit endorsement of "humane" animal exploitation.

Actually, though, the observation is recognition that there is a great deal of suffering in the world, and we each have limited resources to bring to bear against this suffering.

As explained in "Letter to a Young Matt," earlier in my life I didn't understand that suffering was irreducibly bad—full stop. I'm unable to convey this point entirely to most people; luckily, few other people have suffered to the point where they wished they would die.

But knowing what I now know about suffering, my personal goal is to use my life's choices such that the world will have less suffering in it than if I made different choices.

This is not to say that I don't care about justice, or that I am indifferent to exploitation.

It isn't that I care about a chicken more than an innocent person imprisoned; I don't have a greater affinity for a pig than a starving child.

But time and resources are limited. What I do with my finite life is the result of a simple calculation: Lessen the amount of suffering in the world as much as possible.

Full stop.

If I were to spend my time advocating for a victim of tribal violence, or a mutilated woman in a sexist country, or a macaque in a lab, or an elephant maimed by poachers, or a dog in a shelter, I could potentially reduce the horribly heartbreaking and utterly compelling suffering these individuals experience.

But—and this is a lesson it took me years to learn—when I choose to do one thing, I'm choosing not to do another.

And if, at this point in history, I work on an issue other than farmed animal advocacy, the net result would be more suffering in the world.

If agribusiness weren't causing such intense suffering for so many farmed animals, then I would be compelled to work on a different, tractable issue that was creating more suffering. Otherwise, there would be more net suffering in the world.

I realize this is not how most people make their choices. Nearly everyone cares most about what is closest to him—genetically, geographically. And most of the rest have a pet project, based on personal affinity for a specific issue or species.

That is why it is absolutely and utterly urgent that the rest of us focus our choices—our limited time and resources—on reducing suffering as much as possible.

II.

BEING

VEGAN

On Living with Compassion

This piece was initially published as
"On Being Vegan" in 1995.

> Cowardice asks the question, "Is it safe?"
> Expediency asks the question, "Is it politic?"
> Vanity asks the question, "Is it popular?"
> But conscience asks the question, "Is it right?"
> And there comes a point when one must take a position
> that is neither safe, nor politic, nor popular, but one
> must take it because one's conscience tells one that
> it is right.
>
> —*Martin Luther King, Jr.*

What we choose to eat makes a powerful statement about our ethics and our view of the world—about our very humanity. By not buying meat, eggs, and dairy products, we withdraw our support from cruelty to animals, undertake an economic boycott of factory farms, and support the production of cruelty-free foods.

Choosing to act with compassion is a potent public affirmation of our character. From children and athletes to celebrities and grandparents, compassionate living is spreading—and easier than ever! Today, even small-town grocery stores can feature a variety of veggie burgers, dogs, deli slices, plant-based milks, nondairy desserts—a bounty unimaginable only a decade or two ago!

OPPOSING CRUELTY: A RESULTS-BASED APPROACH

When you first discover the reality of modern animal agriculture, avoiding all products from factory farms might seem too big a change. But don't be overwhelmed; just take small steps. For example, you could eliminate meat from certain meals or on certain days. As you get used to eating less meat and find alternatives you enjoy, it may become easier to eliminate meat altogether.

At some point, you might decide to try to root out every product associated with modern animal agriculture. But some type of connection can be found everywhere if one looks hard enough. Some examples are organic foods (manure used as fertilizer), bicycles (animal fat used in the vulcanization of tires), books (hooves and bones in binding glue), roads and buildings (animal products used in curing concrete), and even water (bone char used for filtration by some water treatment plants; water itself has been "tested on animals").

Ultimately, living with compassion means striving to maximize the good we accomplish, not following a set of rules or trying to fit a certain label. From eating less meat to being vegan, our actions are only a means to an end: decreasing suffering.

For this reason, we believe the consequences of our actions should guide our choices. Oftentimes, there's more to consider than whether or not an item is completely animal-free. For example, it can be prohibitively expensive and extremely time-consuming to try to shun every minor or hidden animal-derived ingredient. More importantly, avoiding an ever-increasing list of these ingredients can make us appear obsessive and lead others to believe that compassionate living is impossible. This defeats our purpose: ending cruelty to animals!

Our desire to oppose and help end cruelty to animals can guide our choices, as well as provide a simple, easy-to-understand explanation of our actions. The question isn't, "Is this vegan?" but rather, "What is best for preventing suffering?"

DEALING WITH OTHERS

When you share your new discoveries and ideas, some friends and family members may not only show resistance, they might even react with mockery or anger. In order to prevent suffering, however, we must let our compassion for animals shine through the pain and anger we feel about what happens to them in factory farms and industrial slaughterhouses. Unless others can respect us—as opposed to finding us self-righteous and judgmental—they will have little interest in taking steps to end cruelty to animals.

Instead of expecting others to change immediately, we need to be understanding, giving everyone time and space to consider the realities of factory farms at their own pace and within their unique situation. Burning bridges with judgment and anger only serves to create enemies and feed the stereotype that vegans are self-righteous.

Although it may be tempting to get into arguments—for example, about our prehistoric ancestors' diet, the relative importance of antioxidants—the simplest statement can be the most powerful: "I know that I don't want to suffer. Therefore, I don't want to cause others to suffer."

As long as we remain respectful, our positive example and the information we provide will ultimately be the best voice for the animals.

How Vegan?
Ingredients vs. Results

Vegan Outreach Web site, June 1998

When I first got actively involved in animal rights around 1990, "How vegan?" had a simple answer: Either something is vegan or it isn't. The way to tell was to compare all of the ingredients on every product against lists of all possible animal products. This list eventually became a book, *Animal Ingredients A to Z*, which for years was the best-selling book at Vegan.com.

This simple means of defining "good" and "bad" attracted many of us because it was so straightforward. But even before the list began to grow into an encyclopedia, it was inconsistent. The production of honey kills some insects, but so does driving (and sometimes even walking) and harvesting foods. Many soaps contain stearates, but the tires on cars and bicycles contain similar animal products. Some sugar is processed with bone char, but so is much municipal water. Adding "not tested on animals" to the definition of vegan added a whole new level of complexity.

Still, it can be difficult to give up a black-and-white set of rules. Over the years, people have added "exceptions," definitions of "necessity," or claims of "intention" to save the laundry-list approach. But trying to have a hard definition of what is "vegan" is, ultimately, arbitrary. The production of organic vegetables often uses manure; the production of "veganic" food injures and kills animals during planting, harvesting, and transport.

Of course, we could all "do no harm" by committing suicide and letting our bodies decompose in a forest. But short of this, the best path is to take a step back and consider why we really care whether something is vegan.

EFFECTIVE ADVOCACY

The question of "How vegan?" is important not for us, but because raising and slaughtering animals for food is, by far, the most significant cause of suffering today, both in terms of the numbers and the level of cruelty inflicted.

Knowing this, the issue for thoughtful, compassionate people isn't, "Is this vegan?" Rather, the important question is this: "Which choice leads to less suffering?" Our guide shouldn't be someone's endless list of ingredients, but rather doing our absolute best to stop cruelty to animals. Veganism is important not as an end in itself, but as a powerful tool for opposing the horrors of factory farms and industrial slaughterhouses.

This moves the discussion away from finding a definition or avoiding a certain product and into the realm of effective advocacy—advocacy in the broadest sense, in every aspect of our lives. In other words, the focus isn't so much our personal beliefs or specific choices, but rather the animals and their suffering.

If we believe that being vegan is important, we must recognize that being an effective advocate for the animals is far more important! The impact of our individual veganism—several hundred land animals over the course of a lifetime—pales in comparison to what we have the potential to accomplish with our example. For every single person inspired to change their habits, the impact we have on the world doubles!

Conversely, for every person we convince that veganism is overly demanding by obsessing with an ever-increasing list of ingredients, we do worse than nothing: We turn someone away who could have made a real difference for animals if they hadn't met us! Currently, the vast majority of people in our society have no problem eating an actual chicken's leg. It is not surprising that many people dismiss vegans as unreasonable and irrational when our example includes interrogating waiters, not eating veggie burgers cooked on the same grill with meat, condemning medicines, etc.

Instead of spending our limited time and resources worrying about the margins (cane sugar, drugs), our focus should be on increasing our impact every day. Helping just one person change leads to hundreds fewer animals suffering in factory farms. By choosing to promote compassionate eating, every person we meet is a potential major victory.

HARD QUESTIONS AND RESULTS

Admittedly, taking a results-based view of veganism is not as straightforward as consulting a list. Areas of concern range from the example we set to the allocation of resources, asking questions such as: Do I bother asking for an ingredient list when eating out with non-veg friends and family, perhaps ending up not eating anything, and risk making veganism appear irrational and impossible? Also: How should I spend or donate my limited money and time?

Situations are subtle and opportunities unique; thus, there can be no set, easy answers. But if our decisions are guided by a desire to accomplish the most good, we each have enormous potential to create change.

It is not enough to be a righteous vegan, or even a dedicated, knowledgeable vegan advocate. The animals don't need us to be right, they need us to be effective. In other words, we don't want to simply win an argument with a meat eater, we want to open people's hearts and minds to a more compassionate lifestyle.

To do this, we have to be the opposite of the vegan stereotype. Regardless of the sorrow and outrage we rightly feel at the cruelties the animals suffer, we must strive to be what others want to be: joyful, respectful individuals whose fulfilling lives inspire others. Only then can we do our best for the animals.

More on Being Vegan

Vegan Outreach Web site, September 2013

When we discover how animals are really treated on factory farms, it is entirely human to react with revulsion and disgust, wanting to cut all connection to these horrors. This can easily become an endless quest, however; if you look long enough, everything we do in society has some connection to animal exploitation.

Seeking new connections to animal exploitation is relatively easy. It is much more difficult to put aside our visceral repulsion and, instead of striving to avoid personal contamination, work to change society as much as possible. Doing our best to expose and end modern agribusiness' brutality requires that we use our very limited time and resources in a manner entirely different than trying to be ever more "vegan." Rather than removing ourselves as far as possible from a world filled with animal cruelty, we must be fully engaged in the world, so we can save as many animals as possible from the horrors of factory farms. We must engage with people where they are—not where we are or where we want them to be—in order to open their hearts and minds to the animals' plight.

In his interview with Vegan.com's Erik Marcus, author Jonathan Safran Foer explained the two motivations for his book *Eating Animals*: to be useful (not thorough), and to get people to focus on the first step, not the last.

Yes! This is it exactly!

Every time we focus on our current personal choices—rather than the animals' obvious suffering—we lose the opportunity to open more hearts and minds and remove support for factory farming. Every time we make the issue about our current personal definition of "vegan"—for example, a real "vegan" shouldn't take medicine because it has been tested on animals and/or contains an "animal product"—we reinforce the stereotype of vegans as fanatics and veganism as dogma. This actively hurts animals.

We may sincerely believe our current personal level of purity to be the only honorable and coherent position. But the animals suffering today don't need consistent principles or unadulterated products. They don't need us to avoid every minor ingredient or promote a "perfect" philosophy.

Desperately and immediately, the animals need us to be pragmatic, optimally effective advocates in our imperfect, inconsistent world. To reach the most new people, our example must be thoughtful, selfless, and joyful. This is the way we can actually help animals the most. The rest is just talk.

Meet the Man Behind Vegan Outreach

Interview with Made Just Right, 2010

Today we're talking to Matt Ball, cofounder of *Vegan Outreach. Since 1993, Matt, as executive director, has grown VO into the leading grassroots animal advocacy organization, with active members across the country and around the world distributing VO's detailed, documented booklets* Why Vegan? Compassionate Choices, *and* Even If You Like Meat, *along with the* Guide to Cruelty-Free Eating.

VO has distributed more than 13,000,000 of these powerful booklets. As Matt said when he was inducted into the Animal Rights Hall of Fame, Vegan Outreach's mission is to make everyone and anyone, in any situation, the most effective advocate for animals possible.

Over the past seventeen years, VO has published some of the most influential essays, including "How Vegan?" and "A Meaningful Life." Matt is also coauthor of The Animal Activist's Handbook.

What's the one food product you can't live without?

You know, there really is no single food that I couldn't do without. There are so many great things out there that if one product were discontinued (or got too expensive), I'd replace it with another. And it might lead me to explore something new—that's happened in the past.

What are some positive changes you've noticed in your health or otherwise that occurred since you started your diet?

My entire life has changed since I went vegan. My career has obviously changed as well, and I've met and had the opportunity to work with some of the most amazing and dedicated people in the world. More importantly, I met Anne Green, my wife of eighteen years, when I was head of the Students for Animal Rights group at the University of Illinois.

What's the most awkward food encounter you've had in relation to your diet?

When I went vegetarian, and then vegan, my family didn't react with, shall we say, the greatest enthusiasm. This was partly my fault. For one, I didn't know nearly enough about nutrition to convince them that I could cut animal products out of my diet and remain healthy. (I'm famous for not liking vegetables.) Second, I initially had the fire of the converted, and was rather angry (and preachy) when others didn't react to the truth of factory farms as I did. It took me quite a while to learn how to deal constructively with situations like that.

"The Fire of the Converted"—a lot of us can relate to that! It was a great idea to write about how to deal with those situations. So, is there any type of situation (e.g., social, survival) that would cause you to cheat on your diet? When?

I'd like to think that over time, my survival is a net good for the animals, so I think I would "cheat" on my diet to survive. But it also depends on what you mean by "cheat." I'll take medicines that have been tested on animals, I'll drink tap water filtered with bone char, I'll eat a veggie burger cooked in a non-vegan restaurant—all things that some vegans consider to be "non-vegan."

But to me, "vegan" isn't a diet or a set of rules or exclusions. Rather, my veganism is about trying to reduce as much suffering in the world as possible. To do so requires more than just making the right purchases; it also requires being an example that leads to more people changing their habits and diets.

It's your last day on Earth and you can eat anything you want for your final meal. What would it be?

The veg sampler plate from the Ethiopian restaurant Meskerem in Washington, DC. It would have to be delivered, though, because I'd want to spend the day at home with Anne and Ellen.

Do you think this is a diet that everyone in the world needs to adopt, or are we better off with only a portion of the population following it?

The world would be unbelievably better if, instead of viewing them as food, everyone respected other animals as the individuals they are, whose lives matter to them.

If you could make everyone do just one thing that would advance the vegan cause, what would that thing it be?

I'd just want people to have full knowledge of the hidden reality behind their food choices, so they aren't making decisions based on agribusiness' lies. I'd want everyone to work in a chicken farm and a slaughterhouse, so they could really experience the horrors.

Want to Help Animals? No Vegan Extremism Required

Q&A with NPR, March 2013

Do vegans who insist that such medicines or medical products should be refused by other vegans undermine what VO tries to accomplish, and if so, in what specific ways?

Every time we focus on the undeniable suffering of animals on factory farms—rather than making the issue about our personal choices/definitions/labels/philosophy—the world is a better place. This is something that took me years to discover; initially, my veganism was all about how "dedicated" and "consistent" I was. Everything centered on how committed I was/how amazing my veganism was, not on the animals, nor on helping them as much as possible.

Being an effective advocate for the animals—including being a positive, practical example—is much more difficult than memorizing a list of animal ingredients. But if we really oppose cruelty to animals, we need to do everything we can to end factory farms, even if that is more difficult than personally being ever more "vegan."

The good thing, though, is that today the "vegan police"/ingredient-obsessed and "consistency"-obsessed types are an incredibly tiny minority, compared to all the pragmatic activists who are focused on the animals. The vegan police may be loud in some circles (and featured in news reports that seek to ridicule those concerned for animals), but they aren't impeding the progress the rest of us are making in changing people's minds about eating animals, nor are they preventing the abolition of modern agribusiness' worst abuses.

Is a person a better, more committed vegan when s/he refuses medicines or medical products that include animal products?

A few decades ago, I thought a person's dedication was measured by how much they "gave up"—how hard their life seemed relative to mine. It took me a while to realize the question isn't how "vegan" anyone is; rather, the only issue is the animals' suffering.

All that matters is the impact we have for the animals in the real world. What we personally consume (especially at the margins) is almost irrelevant compared to what we can accomplish with thoughtful, honest advocacy for the animals. For example, influencing just one person to stop eating chickens and eggs—or even simply cutting back!—has an almost infinitely larger impact than if I avoid yet another obscure, minuscule animal product.

Specific to medicine: I'm alive and functioning today because of "non-vegan" medicines. Modern medicine saved my life again this year. Last year, it saved a friend and colleague. This is also true for many of the people who are doing the most good today. The point isn't to suffer to be "vegan." The point is to lead a meaningful life that reduces as much suffering as possible, making the world a better place than if we hadn't existed.

Dealing with Vegans

Response to Vegan Outreach member, 2013

I'm not 100 percent vegan myself. I remember talking to you about this issue before, and you told me that it was better for a person to do the best he/she could rather than try to obtain some sort of personal purity. I really liked your approach.

[I joined] a Facebook group of [certain] vegans. I used to be more active, but I have largely stayed away from it lately, as there are too many humongous egos there that are complete turnoffs. They are militant vegans who even go as far as to add the word "vegan" to their names. I won't dare to even mention that I have honey sometimes, as I know I will be bashed. . . . Never mind the fact that I've helped several people become vegetarian, I will still be hated for being 99 percent vegan rather than 100 percent. They were recently bashing Alicia Silverstone for "making a mockery out of veganism." It's some kind of angry elitist purity club going on, which is a complete turnoff.

If you have any words of advice from your years of experience as a vegan, maybe it could help them. There are currently over 1,700 people on this Facebook group, *yet they just need some insight and guidance, as they are wasting efforts on massive EGO battles. Thanks so much for all that you do!*

This will seem to be a cop-out, but it is based on hard-won insights from over two decades of being vegan: Don't worry about the egotistical folk on the Internet. There are many fanatical vegans who will shout-down anyone who might disagree on anything. The chances of them changing are very small, and the frustration caused by interacting with them is very high.

More importantly, we have limited time and resources—both emotional and monetary. The animals are much better served when we spend our limited time and resources reaching out to new people who don't know about factory farms and the compassionate alternatives, rather than beating our head against the wall of arrogant vegans who are only concerned with personal purity and validation.

P.S.—I love the description of the group, which is basically "Let's make the world vegan! Non-vegans aren't welcome." Is there a better example of preferring a vegan club to a vegan world?

"Why Don't You Promote My Diet?"

2012

Vegan Outreach often receives criticism that the meal examples/food items we mention in our publications don't measure up. We should promote only whole foods, or raw foods, or cheap foods, or organic/veganic foods, or local foods, or foods sold at vegan-only stores, etc.

As you know, validating or promoting a specific diet isn't Vegan Outreach's purpose. Rather, we seek to reduce as much suffering as possible. People who currently eat animals are the only ones in a position to make changes that help reduce suffering.

Therefore, the information in our booklets and on our main Web site is primarily aimed at meat eaters who might be willing and able to consider making changes. There is no point in showing people the revolting hidden horrors of modern agribusiness if the alternative seems unappealing and/or so strange as to be beyond consideration.

As mentioned before, we are asking people to take the first step, rather than promoting the last step. To this end, the information we present seeks to be useful, rather than thorough.

Simple, Familiar, Tasty— for the Animals!

Why Vegan Outreach Blog, September 2013

There are many (many) vegans who think a "vegan" dish has to be fat-free and/or gluten-free and/or raw and/or local and/or locally sourced and/or exotic and/or veganic and/or entirely made of vegetables. And, of course, hyperhealthy and not within twelve miles of a GMO. Look at the ingredient list and the time required to prepare many vegan recipes.

Compare the pictures of many vegan recipes to what big, successful companies use to sell their food/promote their restaurants.

The narrow attitude of some vegans reinforces the public's notion that vegan food requires intense commitment and mythical alchemy—all for food that is unfamiliar and/or taste-free. But eating vegan isn't rocket science: Anything and everything counts, as long as it isn't from an animal!

Yes, that's right—even if it is familiar and tasty!

And the psychology of helping animals isn't difficult to understand, either: To help animals, we need to convince those whose choices currently hurt animals to make different choices. The more we ask of those people, though, the fewer of them will change.

In other words, every time we focus on anything other than the animals, the fewer people who change, and the more animals suffer.

So, viva easy, familiar, tasty vegan food—for the animals!

Clubs, Soy, and the Choice We Face

Why Vegan Outreach Blog, July 2013

Nearly twenty years ago, Jack Norris summed it up well: "We want a vegan world, not a vegan club."

This may seem obvious, but the implications are significant. If a vegan world really is our goal, we can't spend our time talking back and forth with other vegans about how great we are, how amazing veganism is, how so-and-so isn't really vegan.

Rather, we have to use our limited time and resources to convince more and more meat eaters to take steps to help animals.

These are two very different discussions. Although many vegans care about any health claim regarding meat, far-reaching environmental issues, and any and every connection to animal exploitation, this is simply not the case for the vast majority of non-vegans. Go to any McDonald's or a grocery store or mall food court—people aren't making their choices for optimal nutrition (or optimal anything). They are choosing what is familiar, convenient, cheap, and tasty.

For all intents and purposes, modern animal agribusiness doesn't care about a handful of whole-food, locavore, hardcore vegans. Big ag knows that although this is a profitable sidebar at Whole Foods, it isn't the future for the masses. And for every person who goes entirely vegan because of health concerns, many more give up eating large animals and start consuming many more smaller, more intensively raised animals.

What actually is a threat to entrenched interests are psychologically informed campaigns that accept human nature as it is and work within our current system—for example, meat reduction (Meatless Mondays) and cruelty-free foods that are familiar, convenient, cheap, and tasty.

To fend off the latter, there is a concerted effort by big agribusiness companies to attack soy, which is the basis for most successful veg meats. It is a transparent ploy by the meat industry, but surprisingly effective—aided by a subset of vegans who are quick to believe any negative claim about any food. If you know someone who has bought into the meat industry's attacks, send them Virginia Messina RD's summary[1] of health research regarding soy and Jack's reply[2] to one of the hatchet jobs on soy.

In the end, we each need to make a choice: Do we spend our limited time glorifying and defending our specific veganism (and any other food and political obsessions we insist on attaching), or do we do realistic work that will actually help animals and move us toward a vegan world?

---

1 Virginia Messina, "Is It Safe to Eat Soy Foods?" Vegetarian Diets: A Dietitian's Guide, 2014: www.vegnutrition.com/soy/index.html.

2 Jack Norris, "Response to Not Soy Fast," JackNorrisRD.com, April 5, 2011: http://jacknorrisrd.com/response-to-not-soy-fast/

Let Them Eat Cake

2011 Online Chat with AR Zone

You and your wife have raised your child as a vegan from birth. Could you tell us some of the hurdles you found difficult to get over, and offer any advice to those of us trying to accomplish the same now?

I would hope that the situation is different and easier today than it was in 1994! Raising Ellen really didn't have a lot of hurdles, at least regarding veganism. People asked us questions, and we answered. We had done our research and knew more about nutrition than our interrogators. And the people who were belligerent we just ignored. (Oddly, the question we got over and over and over was, "But what about birthday parties?" It was as though everyone's only memory of childhood was eating cake and ice cream. It was crazy.)

Here are the main pieces of advice I'd give:

1. Know your nutrition. Not from propaganda that seeks to glorify a certain diet, but from

legitimate, impartial sources whose main goal is an honest and thorough evaluation.
2. Take advantage of the community—there were no vegan parenting boards on the Web in 1993/94.
3. Don't let the haters get to you.

I think the last part is key for any vegan in any situation. I understand taking attacks/ignorance personally; it is so hard not to, especially when it comes to the welfare of your child. And I sure identify with the desire to be able to "win an argument" with a meat eater. But the reality is that there are some people who will be belligerent regardless of what we say.

I think we will all be happier—and thus better examples and advocates for the animals—if we accept that some people will just be jerks. (And let's be honest, that's true about vegans, too. There are vegans who will be loudly belligerent with anyone whose thoughts deviate ever so slightly from theirs.) On the other hand, loads of people are initially hostile but come around when treated with respect.

If a member of the public asked you whether veganism was easy or hard, how would you respond?

I would say that if you are currently following the standard American diet and don't have close vegan friends, the idea of being vegan/going vegan immediately will almost certainly seem hard. If the situation were right, I would go on to say this: If you are committed and resourceful, it will definitely get easier and easier (especially with things like Gardein Tuscan chick'n breasts).

For us now, after being vegan for decades, eating this way is second nature, so much so that when people say "Veganism is so hard," our involuntary initial reaction is "What the heck are you talking about?" That isn't the right response, obviously. It took me a long time to get to this point (and I still sometimes forget), but questions from the public aren't for me; I'm answering for the animals.

Of course, I, like nearly everyone, like to talk about myself. It is nearly irresistible! But the animals have no voice but ours. So every question we get is an opportunity to answer for the animals. In this case, the issue isn't my opinion of veganism. Rather, I think about where the other person is coming from. If I say veganism is easy, and they think "Well, maybe for you, but it seems too hard to me!" they're lost to making changes for the animals. So the point isn't to show how into veganism I am, how much I know, how easy it is for me, or even what it will be like for them in X months. Rather, the goal should be to engage the person from where they are at the moment.

Veganism is getting lots of media attention lately. Oprah Winfrey just did a big Vegan Challenge and Kathy Freston's Veganist *[was] #1 on Amazon. With the "v-word" finally gaining mainstream recognition, why is it that some activists and organizations are choosing this point in time to shy away from using it?*

For example, one advocate has said the following: "My long experience shows the word vegan *scares many people, but the word* vegetarian *interests them. We also see this overwhelmingly when leafleting—people want vegetarian information far more than vegan information. Ironically, I'll bet we get far fewer vegans by using the word* vegan, *since many vegetarians do go vegan once they see how easy it is and start down the path of compassionate eating."*

Thanks for this important question—it brings up a key aspect of Vegan Outreach.

I understand the personal pride that many vegans feel when "vegan" gets mentioned in the media, and when famous people endorse it. But VO doesn't exist to promote the word "vegan," to celebrate veganism, or to get media attention. Rather, our goal is to reduce as much suffering as possible. As we wrote elsewhere:

> We must honestly evaluate the world as it currently is, and then do our very best to reduce as much suffering as possible.
>
> We must reach and influence the people who might be willing to go vegan; reach and influence people who might be willing to go vegetarian; reach and influence the people who won't (now) go veg, but who might stop buying meat from factory farms . . . and help support all of these people as they continue to evolve as consumers.

Outreach efforts to all of these people are necessary if we are to help a large and diverse society evolve to a new ethical norm.[1]

So we don't want to limit ourselves only to the audience that is currently receptive to veganism. Rather, we want to maximize the impact we have for the animals everywhere as much as possible.

Two last things: First, I think we might be making a mistake if we make too much of rich and powerful people talking about veganism. So many vegans went overboard when Oprah first talked about veganism, but despite being immensely rich and powerful, she was back eating chickens soon thereafter. Second, and tangentially related, overall the "health argument" has probably caused more animals to suffer and be slaughtered than anything since the advent of factory farming.

Vegan Outreach advocates for "less suffering." Could you please explain what is meant by "less suffering"? And if it were possible to commodify other animals for our purposes without causing too much suffering, would Vegan Outreach approve of this?

These are either really easy or really difficult questions. We could spend the rest of the day debating the neurol-

---

1 Matt Ball & Jack Norris, "A New World, Piece by Piece," Vegan Outreach eNewsletter, June 27, 2007: www.veganoutreach.org/enewsletter/20070627.html.

ogy and philosophy of suffering, but that really wouldn't be a good use of our limited time—relative to what else we could do, it just wouldn't accomplish anything useful. So let me just say that most people know suffering when they see it. They don't need a PhD to call what happens in the video *Meet Your Meat* "suffering." They don't need to be a neurologist to be repulsed by the footage in *Farm to Fridge*. If we want to make as much progress as we can for the animals, we should start our conversations with obvious suffering, rather than with philosophy or semantics. And obviously, we don't approve of unnecessary suffering, even if someone says it isn't "too much."

In the first entry under "Ethics and Religion" in the FAQs to Vegan Outreach's "Starter Guide" it says this:
   "Why is it wrong to eat meat?"
   "It's not a question of being 'right' or 'wrong.' If one wants fewer animals to suffer and die, then one can stop supporting such practices by not eating animal products."
   Why wouldn't Vegan Outreach state what one can only hope they think is obvious?? It is wrong to eat other animals.

I sympathize with this demand. On the other hand (and, again, this is something that took me many years to realize), what I think or claim or "know" is irrelevant. The only people in a position to save animals in the future are people currently eating meat. So the question isn't if we vegans think something is "right" or "wrong." The only question is: What can we do or say to lead as many meat eaters as possible to start making positive changes for the animals?

(Indeed, it is rather sad to see forlorn vegans sitting around debating words and philosophy among themselves. There is so much actual, constructive work that needs to be done! We don't have time to type away on the Internet to demand satisfaction from other vegans. We need to get real results in the real world for real animals.)

As experience shows and psychological research reinforces, telling people that what they are doing is "wrong" isn't the best way to open their hearts and minds. Erik Marcus has pointed out that agribusiness has hidden behind elaborate illusions; their entire industry is based on lying to consumers. People are making their decisions after having been deceived their entire lives. So instead of telling meat eaters that what they are doing is "wrong," it is both honest and more constructive to point out that they have been lied to their entire lives. People don't like being lied to!

A similar line of reasoning applies to philosophy. Obviously, the vast majority of people believe humans are "superior" to/distinct from (other) animals. But they don't immediately need to accept the idea that other animals have rights or fully internalize a utilitarian worldview to start taking steps that help animals. Joe Espinosa has clearly articulated this when dealing with people, telling them they can believe whatever they want about animals and still find factory farms repulsive and something they don't want to support.

Not to harp on all my mistakes, but my prior attitude of "Just tell everyone the whole truth! They need to know!" was very harmful to the animals. It was psychologically at odds with creating change. But more so, it was just downright stupid, as this attitude ignored how my own views and choices had evolved over time!

How does Vegan Outreach measure the effectiveness of your outreach campaigns? Is it based on X number of booklets handed out so therefore it is X number of people "reached" regardless of whether they read it or not?

This is a complicated question. We know that giving someone a booklet in passing has a much lower chance of changing them than sitting them down, befriending them, getting them to watch *Meet Your Meat*, answering all their questions personally, teaching them how to shop and cook, etc. But for creating widespread change, the latter is not an option.

As Jack Norris points out, spreading veganism is, in the end, a numbers game. We can do what we can to tweak this—focusing on younger people, using a specific booklet for a certain crowd, listening carefully to feedback, studying the most relevant psychological research—but in the end, to change our society we need to get this information to as many people as quickly as possible.

Can you explain why Vegan Outreach uses graphic photos in its booklets?

The short answer is that, based on the experience we've had in the past two decades, using images that show cruelty to animals (as opposed to preaching philosophy, or showing only "happy" pictures) is the most effective means of reducing as much suffering as possible.

There are many factors playing into this. Perhaps the most important is that, while most people are speciesist and think it is OK to kill animals, the vast, vast majority of people oppose cruelty to animals. Showing people the hidden cruelty that goes on in factory farms and industrial slaughterhouses starts where people are—repulsed by cruelty to animals—rather than where we want them to be.

Our impact on the environment is at the forefront of all our minds in the age of climate change. Vegan Outreach says that they give away millions of pamphlets. These are full-color, sixteen-page documents which have to be transported around the country: Isn't there a better way now using the Internet, and thereby reducing VO's carbon footprint?

You're right: The Internet is becoming a hugely important advocacy tool for us to use! And it is amazing. When I met Jack and Anne, e-mail was a complete novelty, and the Web didn't even exist.

But if we want to prevent as much suffering as possible, we need to change society as quickly as possible. To do so, we can't limit ourselves to those who are online, happen across a link, choose to click on the link, and spend the time on the site. We must go beyond this and reach out directly to millions of people—people who wouldn't ever otherwise learn of the animals' urgent plight.

In my experience, the typical response to the horrors of factory farming is to pursue reform ("happy meat") rather than elimination (veganism). Companies are capitalizing on this and the "humane" sector is rapidly growing. Does VO have plans to modify its booklets to more aggressively address so-called "humane" animal products?

This is a great question.

The first aspect of this is "happy meat." Obviously, there are people who do stop supporting factory farms and eat "sustainable" meat. But many vegans read far too much into this. We suffer from availability bias—extrapolating from what we personally see to the population as a whole.[2] The reality, though, is that "happy meat" is an absolutely minuscule market for rich, over-educated Americans. Sadly, rich, overeducated people are vastly overrepresented in the media! And people who excuse eating animals, at any level, are given even more media coverage by their fellow elites.

Of course, I understand the extreme frustration of seeing all this rationalization and glorification of eating animals. In general, though, we vegans massively over-react to it, spending a tremendously disproportionate amount of our limited time and our limited emotional

---

2 Availability bias also has applicability in the vegan community, too, where the loudest, most outspoken—or obnoxious—person seems to represent all vegans. And, of course, the meat-eating media love to promote the angriest, most extreme, obsessive, fanatical vegan as the community's voice. We should be aware of this and try to counter it as best we can.

resources arguing with and being angry at people eating/
promoting "happy meat." There are better uses of our
limited time and resources.

Of course, it is disappointing when people don't go
vegan when they hear our message, or when someone
stops being vegetarian and eats animals again. But let me
tell you from long experience—this isn't because of the
presence of "happy meat."

Obviously, it has always been the case that the vast
majority of people don't change when they learn the case
for vegetarianism. And there have been failed vegetarians ever since there have been vegetarians. Several years
ago, I read a survey showing more former vegetarians in
the United Kingdom than actual vegetarians.

Similarly, when he spent two years leafleting across
the country nearly twenty years ago, Jack felt he met more
former vegetarians than current vegetarians. It wasn't
because of Michael Pollan (author of *The Omnivore's
Dilemma*) or *New York Times* columnist Mark Bittman
or Polyface Farms or Whole Foods. It was because they
didn't feel healthy as a vegetarian.

This trend continues today—just Google "failed vegetarian" or "failed vegan." The Internet gives these people a loud megaphone, and meat eaters give them endless
attention.

We vegans suffer from availability bias regarding the
prevalence of failed vegetarians. We hear from every
single "happy meat" eater, and extrapolate this to the
general population. But as Jack found, there actually is a
real problem here: Many buy into the vegan propaganda
and don't learn honest and thorough nutrition. This

leads to many people going vegetarian with unrealistic expectations (of how easy it will be, of the health benefits they will immediately experience, etc.). That's why Jack became a registered dietician and created www.veganhealth.org. We can do better. We need to do better.

The other aspect of your question is the nature of change, in both individuals and in society. We would, of course, love to design a booklet that persuaded everyone to change, and only change right to being vegan. But real change is rarely, if ever, quick or linear. We owe it to the animals to give up our fantasy of the one perfect "argument," and instead do the best possible work in the real world. Or, to paraphrase Martin Luther King, Jr., the arc of history is long and jagged, but ultimately bends toward justice. We should spend more time bending, rather than despairing over the hiccups.

In "Letter to a Young Matt," you say that when you were twenty-one, you were self-righteous, angry, and obsessive. Since then, you say, you have learned that "what matters is suffering," something your younger self was supposedly ignorant about having not personally suffered. You say you were worried about "abstractions and words and principles" and "argued about exploitation, oppression, liberation, etc." You suggest this means you "didn't take suffering seriously." You said: "Now, knowing what suffering really is, and knowing how much there is in the world, all my previous concerns seem—well, to put it kindly, ridiculous."

Why is talking about exploitation, oppression, and

*liberation (putting it kindly) "ridiculous," and is it not
the case that such concerns are all about suffering?*

I agree! All the words are, ultimately, about suffering.
So no more debates about words, and more actual work
reducing actual suffering!

*In your VO eNewsletter of August 17, 2001, you speak
about a birthday party with a four-year-old child eating a piece of birthday cake. You say: "Our opinion
is—what does a piece of cake at a four-year-old's birthday matter? Are the consequences of her eating it (as
opposed to it being thrown out) worse than the impression it makes on twenty other children (and parents) if
the vegan police grill everyone about the nature of everything with which Ellen comes into contact? In short, we
aren't out to raise an ideologue."*

*Do you think that by showing your position isn't
consistent, and being a "flexible vegan," you could be
confusing others? If the four-year-old were allergic to
dairy, would you be as flexible? If not, why not?*

Good questions! They get to some important distinctions.

I've heard the allergy question before, but for me, it is
not an appropriate analogy. I don't choose to eat vegan
because I physically must. I don't avoid meat, eggs, and
dairy to benefit myself. I make my choices to help the
animals, to lessen the amount of suffering in the world.
In other words, being vegan isn't about me; it is about
the animals. So my choices and example are based on
those criteria.

And consistency is another false concern. I've never met anyone who, honestly, continued to eat animals because they were confused by a vegan's supposed lack of "consistency." What I have seen (and sadly been the cause of) are vegans whose self-righteousness and obsessiveness gave others an excuse to ignore the animals' plight. I only hope that I'm able to undo the damage I did in the past when I made veganism about me, rather than about the animals.

I assume most people reading this believe that what they do with their choices is important. Our choices aren't important because they conform to a certain philosophy or because they meet a certain someone's definition. Rather, the importance comes from our choices' consequences: the actual impact we can have on reducing the animals' suffering.

If I could leave you with only one thought to consider, it would be this: The importance of our individual personal choices is nothing—absolutely nothing—compared to the impact we can have if we live for more than ourselves, dedicated to optimal advocacy. Each of us truly can be extraordinary, if we are dedicated to having the greatest constructive influence possible on others. I see the truth of this every day!

III.

ADVOCACY

Anger, Humor, and Advocacy

Vegan Outreach Web site, 2000

Some people have asked how we can make jokes when the animals are suffering so terribly, when we're supposed to be focused on animal liberation. We believe that having a sense of humor is in the animals' best interest, because not only does it make our example more appealing, it also aids in avoiding burnout. In the cumulative fifty or so years we've been active, Jack Norris, Anne Green, and I have known hundreds of activists who have given up—some of whom have even gone back to eating meat! On the other hand, the most successful activists we've known almost always have a sustaining sense of humor.

As a reaction to what goes on in factory farms and slaughterhouses, very strong feelings are understandable and entirely justified. But I believe that our inability—individually and as a movement—to deal with our anger in a constructive manner is one of the greatest hindrances to the advancement of animal liberation.

Over time, people tend to deal with their anger in different ways. Some take to protesting, some to screaming, hatred, and sarcasm. Others disconnect from society and surround themselves with only like-minded people, seeing society as a large conspiracy against veganism.

I do not believe any of this does much to move society toward being more compassionate.

A different approach is to try to maintain a positive outlook and a sense of humor. This makes it easier to continue in activism and to avoid self-righteous fundamentalism, and it also makes it possible to interact positively and constructively with others.

Unfortunately, there is no easy way to gain and maintain a sense of humor. One suggestion is to always remember your ultimate goal. In my case, it is the alleviation of suffering. If I allow myself to be miserable because of the cruelty in the world, I am adding to the suffering in the world. More importantly, I am saying that unless utopia is instantaneously established, it is not possible to be happy. Thus, my goal is inherently unachievable.

To have any change occur in the world, we need to convince others to think beyond themselves. We must be willing to do the same. Just as we want others to look beyond the short-term satisfaction of following habits and traditions, we need to move past our anger to effective advocacy (i.e., moving from yelling and chanting to constructive educational outreach). If I claim that I can't be happy-—that I am a slave to my situation—how can I expect others to act differently?

It also helps to maintain a historical perspective. I realize I am not the first person to be upset by the state of affairs in the world. I can learn from the mistakes and successes of those who came before me.

Few people come to an enlightened view of the world by themselves and overnight. It took me over a year after my first exposure to the issues to go vegetarian, and even longer after that to go vegan. If I had been treated with disgust and anger because of my close-mindedness and (in retrospect) pathetic rationalizations, I would certainly never have gone veg.

My story is not unique. Not only does it show the shortcomings of anger and the benefits of kindness and patience, it also indicates that you shouldn't give up on friends if they don't react to information as you would like. Shunning friends because they don't immediately adopt your vegan views not only cuts you off from the very people we need to reach, it also perpetuates the stereotype of the joyless fanatic with no life other than complaining.

"Fighting" suffering is not the only way to make a better world; creating happiness and joy as part of a thoughtful, compassionate life filled with constructive advocacy can be an even more powerful tool for creating change.

As long as there is conscious life on Earth, there will be suffering. The question becomes what to do with the existence each of us is given. We can choose to add our own fury and misery to the rest, or we can set an example by simultaneously working constructively to alleviate suffering while leading joyous, meaningful, fulfilled lives.

Being a vegan isn't about deprivation, sobriety, and misery. It's about being fully aware so as to be fully alive.

Rotate the Universe

Stewart Solomon

Why Vegan Outreach blog, December 2013

Matt Ball's "How Vegan Is Enough?" lecture at the 2006 Animal Rights Conference was refreshing. I almost didn't go because I was afraid the answer would be that there was no limit to how vegan one should be, that it might be some fire-and-brimstone speech with someone reciting the entire encyclopedia of animal products. Many people hear about all of these trace animal products and think veganism is beyond impossible.

I remember when one person asked Matt how to convince his brother to go vegan. He'd been at it for years and years to no avail and basically felt like a failure. If he couldn't convert his own brother, he thought, how could he affect anyone else? Matt told him to forget about his brother, that his brother wouldn't turn vegan to spite him, if for no other reason. Matt told him to go to a college campus, a concert, a record store, and hand out literature: "Some of them will read it, become vegetarian or vegan, and you will have saved thousands of lives." I took great comfort in that remark. It was as if a huge burden was suddenly lifted from my shoulders.

I remembered that talk earlier today. I was very tired and my back hurt, but I was able to distribute 750 VO booklets at Pasadena City College. On the drive home I started thinking about an old riddle: How many physicists does it take to change a light bulb?

Two. One to hold the bulb and one to rotate the universe.

I think that holding the light bulb is easy, and rotating the universe is sometimes difficult. However, that light bulb must be changed.

Welfare and Liberation

Vegan Outreach Web site, 2001

Does working for or supporting welfare measures harm the longer-term goal of bringing about liberation?

EXPANDING THE FLOOR OF THE CAGE

The Brazilian Landless Farmers movement has a slogan: "Expand the floor of the cage before you try to break out." It is a way of saying that activists should try to improve the status quo in order to have more room in which to work toward a permanent solution. This belief—that one can support efforts that improve welfare and increase awareness while working for liberation—marks one position within the animal liberation movement, and it is characterized by achievements such as McDonald's recent agreement to improve the treatment of chickens. Another common position is summarized as "rights first, rights only, rights *über alles.*"

THE LESSONS OF HISTORY:
IF ABOLITIONISTS HAD BEEN ABSOLUTISTS

While we all understand the desire to embrace and advocate pure-vegan ideals, this shouldn't stop us from studying the history of social movements and reevaluating our tactics. Successful social movements—abolitionism, women's suffrage, the civil rights movement, the gay rights movement—have pushed for reforming the current system while working toward ultimate goals.

For example, take abolitionism and the subsequent civil rights movement in the United States. They were built through successive improvements in the standing of black Americans. Each improvement, each piecemeal reform, elevated the status of blacks and brought greater confidence and experience to organizers, allowing them to fight for further entitlements. If the movement had rejected all reforms, it's unlikely that it ever could have built enough momentum to succeed. Imagine if Frederick Douglass had argued, "Equal voting rights or no rights at all. Equal representation in government and business, or no representation at all." Imagine if Lincoln had refused to issue the Emancipation Proclamation because it didn't guarantee full suffrage and an end to prejudice or segregation. Douglass, Lincoln, and others were cognizant enough of political realities to see that such positions would alienate the mass of the population, condemning abolition to failure.

The same fate awaits any movement that does not seize reforms and strive to educate when opportunities arise. Absolutist movements attract only those already converted to the cause, and remain confined to a small cadre of dedicated but isolated activists. By settling for "nothing short of total liberation," many groups have condemned themselves to acrimonious anonymity and burnout. They cut themselves off from consideration by the public, and do not provide any incentive for change within the animal industries.

More diverse organizations, on the other hand, have attracted broad memberships of vegetarians and non-vegetarians. They achieve results because they can reach out to individuals and businesses that may not share all of their opinions. These results, in turn, bring in new activists who gain confidence and experience. We should recognize, then, that individuals, businesses, and society progress toward a more compassionate ethic gradually, through successive stages of increased concern for animals.

"IT MUST GET WORSE BEFORE IT GETS BETTER"

Some advocates argue that animal liberation is a unique social justice goal, and they oppose welfare reforms because they believe people will choose not to go vegan if they learn that animals are being treated "better." For example, if the public hears that McDonald's will be getting their eggs from producers that keep their laying hens in bigger cages and no longer force-molt them, fewer people will alter their purchasing patterns than had the agreement not been reached and publicized.

Although this argument may seem to have a certain logic, the evidence indicates that reforms draw the attention of non-vegetarians to the issue, persuading many to reconsider their ethics and actions. Animal groups then use these victories to gain visibility and push for further reforms. In this way, welfare measures tend to be a slippery slope toward abolition, not away from it.

European countries—particularly the United Kingdom—are a counterexample to the "it must get worse before it gets better" argument. Animals are treated far better there, and vegetarianism is more widespread. There are more vegetarian restaurants, and non-vegetarian restaurants have more vegetarian options. The advances in animal welfare have given both the UK welfare movement and vegetarian movement confidence and momentum. And the attention paid to animal welfare in business practices and legislation has increased the public's interest in how their food is produced.

The same could become true in the United States. Reforming a company like McDonald's can initiate a domino effect throughout the industry. Competitors now have a greater incentive to match and exceed McDonald's reforms, thereby forcing industry-wide improvements in the living and dying conditions for all animals. No company wants to be singled out as the "cruel one" by a widespread and well-supported campaign.

More importantly, when the industries that rely on animal exploitation raise the issue of humane treatment, it receives far more serious consideration from the public than animal advocates and partisans could ever hope to achieve alone. Once the companies themselves grant that animals have interests at all, it becomes harder to justify using them for food, regardless of specific conditions.

We have sympathy for those who believe McDonald's is the "enemy," and claim we have to "destroy them." But McDonald's is simply the embodiment of consumer demand. Vilifying a faceless corporate entity as the antagonist distracts from what should be the core concern (the suffering of animals) and from the root cause of this suffering (the choices of consumers).

Obviously, McDonald's is not going to become vegan tomorrow. In the meantime, we can help lessen animals' suffering by supporting reforms and consumer education while simultaneously advancing abolition by promoting veganism. If we target non-vegan companies no matter what, they have no incentive to change their farming practices or add more vegan alternatives to their menus. This leads to more suffering, and more difficulty in people going veg.

PURITY OR PROGRESS?

Why else would we oppose welfare reforms? Perhaps so as not to "compromise our principles." But this isn't the case unless our guiding principle is, "Never, under any circumstances, work with non-vegan people or businesses." Why would someone hold that principle above all else, especially when it is at odds with another that seems more fundamental and defensible: "Work to reduce animal suffering"?

Of course, this is not to say that everyone should pursue welfarist measures. Given the current allocation of resources, we believe that the way to lessen the most suf-

fering in the most expedient and ⁄
promote vegetarianism and vega

CONCLUSIONS

If you were being tortured twenty-four hours a ⌐ᵧ
prison cell, would you want an absolutist on your side?
Would you ask that no one on the outside try to stop
your torture because it must be "freedom or nothing at
all"? Would you believe that the worse your treatment
and the greater your suffering, the closer you would be
to freedom? Or would you prefer that someone bring to
light your circumstances and enact reforms that could
significantly reduce your suffering, while also working
toward your liberation?

While our ultimate goal is to end animal exploitation, we must support the reduction of suffering as much
as possible along the way. We should encourage any
action that will help animals, even if all it does is make
their lives a bit less miserable or their deaths a bit less
cruel. We don't stop there, of course, but we can't pass
up the chance to make improvements for animals simply
because it's not enough.

bike and use the money you save to get booklets into more people's hands, leading to more vegetarians and reducing the number of animals who are factory farmed.

Given the reality of our world—the widespread injustices and the tremendous demands on our very limited time and resources—nearly every choice we face offers us imperfect options.

This issue came up most recently when several people took issue with a Product of the Week item in VO's weekly eNewsletter, which mentioned the availability of Lightlife's BBQ at Walmart. Pointing out that a vegan product is available at a certain store isn't, of course, an endorsement of that store. Rather, it is a recognition that not everyone lives near a co-op or Whole Foods (indeed, we have received complaints from other members that some products we mention and some of the ingredients we use in our recipes aren't available in their community).

It is a simple fact: The more widely available vegan products are, the lower their price will be, and the easier it will be for more people to change their diet and maintain that change.

This is how we'll help animals. This is how the world will change.

As much as we'd like to believe that everyone should pay any price and go to any length to be vegetarian, we realize that cost and convenience are determining factors for many, if not most, people. As more people become vegetarian, more large corporations will market meat-free products; it is the nature of a capitalist economy. This doesn't mean current vegans need to change where they shop, what they buy, or the other campaigns they support. But we do need to recognize that, in this imperfect world, it is, overall, a good thing for the animals that big corporations embrace and expand the burgeoning vegetarian market.

It is entirely understandable to want others to adopt not only our diet, but our political, social, and economic views: "It's all connected!" Nearly every activist, at some point, has the idea of creating a grand progressive alliance that promotes veganism, strong environmental protection, sustainability, and fair trade. But these coalitions never get beyond the "should" stage, and factory farming has continued to expand.

It is not unreasonable to believe that the suffering of "farmed" animals is so great, so unnecessary, and so clearly, unequivocally, and indefensibly wrong that we should always keep the focus on the animals. People are looking for a reason to ignore the cruelties of factory farming and the ethical imperative of changing their diet. No one sits around thinking, "Wow, I really want to give up all my favorite foods and be different from my friends and family!"

We are the animals' only voice. If we want to have the greatest impact for these animals, we should not give anyone any excuse to ignore the terrible and unnecessary suffering the animals go through on factory farms and in slaughterhouses.

FROM Advocacy for the Greatest Good

Compassionate Action for Animals' "Their Lives, Our Voices" Conference, 2008

We're all aware of the many, many different forms of animal exploitation that could use our limited time and money.

I've heard many an activist say that they can't turn their back on the circus coming to town, skip a protest at a local lab, or stop volunteering at the animal shelter. Before founding Vegan Outreach, Jack Norris and I pursued many and various methods of advocacy: letter writing campaigns, scores of protests, including civil disobedience. But every time we choose to do one thing, we are choosing not to do another. There is no way around it. We can't do everything. We must—and do—choose.

Given all this, how can we make choices that maximize the amount of good we can accomplish with our limited time and money?

The first and most important step is to set aside our personal biases and needs and instead seek out what is fundamentally important: our first principle. Previously, I discussed at length how suffering is irreducibly bad, and eliminating suffering is fundamentally good. This is Vegan Outreach's first principle, our bottom line and guide: eliminating as much suffering as possible. Everything we do derives directly from that: We make our choices based on which option will lead to the least amount of suffering.

WHY VEGAN OUTREACH?

Based entirely on this first principle, we choose to focus on exposing the cruelties of factory farms and industrial slaughterhouses, while providing honest information about how to pursue a cruelty-free lifestyle. Let me repeat, our emphasis on ethical eating is derived from our first principle, not vice versa. No specific diet has any value in and of itself. Rather, the importance of promoting cruelty-free eating is that it allows us to have the maximum impact on the amount of suffering in the world. There are three reasons for this.

The first reason is that the number of animals raised and killed for food each year in the United States alone vastly exceeds any other form of exploitation, involving numbers far greater than the total human population of the entire world. About ninety-nine out of every hundred animals killed in the United States each year are slaughtered to be eaten.

Of course, if these billions of animals lived happy, healthy lives and had quick, painless deaths, then our concern for suffering would lead us to use our limited time and resources elsewhere. But animals raised for food must endure unfathomable suffering.

Most advocacy tends to revolve around detailed stories of individuals, and the story of any individual chicken, pig, or veal calf clearly rivals any other case of cruelty. Indeed, every year, hundreds of millions of farmed animals—many times more than the total number killed for fur, in shelters, and in laboratories combined—don't even make it to slaughter. They actually suffer to death.

And yet, if we couldn't do anything for these animals, if their lives were beyond our influence, then we would need to have a different focus. But promoting vegetarianism is the most straightforward way we have to reduce suffering. It doesn't require forming a group, or electing a new government, or organizing a major campaign. Instead, we have opportunities every day, because every single person we meet makes decisions that affect the lives of these farmed animals. Inspiring any of these people to change leads to fewer animals suffering on factory farms. Merely convincing one person to go vegetarian spares hundreds and hundreds of animals from the vicious brutalities of modern agribusiness. Many major national campaigns spend huge amounts of time and money for less payoff. By choosing to promote cruelty-free living, every person we meet is a potential major victory.

WHAT AND WHY?

For these reasons, Vegan Outreach works to change as many people's diets as possible per dollar donated and hour worked. We believe the way to accomplish this is to present the optimal message to our target audience. This leads to two obvious questions: Who is our audience, and what is the message that will elicit the greatest change?

With infinite resources, we could reach out to everyone. Given our current reality, though, the goal of maximum change leads Vegan Outreach to focus primarily on students (especially college-aged) in North America.

Of course, not every student is willing to stop eating meat. But relative to the population as a whole, college students tend to be more open-minded—even rebellious against the status quo—and in a position where they aren't as restricted by parents, tradition, and habits. Even if students and senior citizens were equally open to change, students can save more animals over the course of their lives. Young people not only have more meals ahead of them, but they also have more opportunities to influence others.

Also, college students are typically easier to reach. For a relatively small investment of time, an activist can hand a copy of *Even If You Like Meat* or *Compassionate Choices* to hundreds of students who otherwise may have never viewed a full and compelling case for ethical eating.

Because we take suffering seriously, the message we choose to present to this audience is the cruelty to animals on factory farms and in industrial slaughterhouses. We have found this simple and straightforward message to have many benefits, including honesty and strength of motivation.

However, many new vegetarians think, "Even though I care about animals, other people won't. People are selfish; I'll appeal to their self-interest!" But look around. Is, for example, the "selfish" health argument working? For years we've known that being obese is an incredible threat to good health, yet every year, more and more people in the United States become more and more overweight! Is this really the message with the best chance to create real and lasting change for the animals?

Also, we don't want to get people to just consider changing their diet. We want them to change, maintain that change, and advocate change. If someone gives up meat to improve their health, the next time they hear someone praise a different diet, that same person might switch and end up eating even more animals than before! So we should try to get people to choose compassion for reasons that are sustainable.

I'm not fooling myself. I know that exposing what goes on in factory farms and slaughterhouses isn't going to reach everyone. But feel-good arguments that avoid the horrors of meat production are easily dismissed. They are simply not compelling enough for the majority of the population (especially young people). We don't want people to nod in agreement and continue on as before. It is far better if, today, 95 percent of people turn away revolted and 5 percent consider the animals' plight than if everyone smiles politely and continues on to McDonald's for a "healthy" chicken sandwich or salad.

Let me repeat: Trying to appeal to everyone hasn't worked, and it won't work at this time. It is well past time to give up the fantasy that there is some perfect self-centered argument that will magically compel everyone to change.

Conversely, showing people what is hidden behind the walls of factory farms and slaughterhouses does work! At Vegan Outreach, we have found cruelty to animals to be the most compelling reason for people to change their diet in a way that actually helps animals—and maintain and promote that change—in the face of peer pressure, tradition, and the latest fad. In the mid-1990s, Jack Norris leafleted colleges around the country. He found a great willingness among students to take and consider information about the realities of modern animal agribusiness and the compassionate alternative. Since then, many hundreds of other activists have found the same. We constantly receive feedback like, "I had no idea what went on! Thank you so much for opening my eyes!"

And yet, there are many, many more people to reach. The simplest way to get booklets to interested people is to stock displays in your area: libraries, music and bookstores, co-ops and natural food stores, coffeehouses, and sympathetic restaurants are possible venues.

Outreach to young people, though, is where the animals get the biggest bang for the buck. Vegan Outreach's Adopt a College program, where activists leaflet at local campuses, concerts, and other venues, serves to reach out methodically to our prime audience. Activists go directly to individuals—people who may never otherwise learn the realities of modern agribusiness and the compassionate alternative—and provide them with illustrated, detailed, and documented information. This is the first systematic plan for bringing about animal liberation by going directly to our most receptive audience.

We know this works, and you can join with the others who are taking part in this powerful, effective activism. You don't need to start a group, or publish a Web site, or organize anything. You just need to take suffering seriously and choose to commit your time, and we'll provide all the materials and guidance you need.

POTENTIAL PITFALLS

When striving to be the best possible advocate, there are a number of pitfalls we need to keep in mind.

We must always remember that people are generally looking for a reason to ignore us. No one sits around thinking, "Wow, I want to give up my favorite foods and be different from my friends and family!" Anyone who has been vegetarian for more than a few minutes knows the many roadblocks—habit, tradition, convenience, taste, familiarity, peer pressure—that keep people from opening their hearts and minds to the animals' plight. Knowing this, we can't give anyone any reasons to ignore the terrible and unnecessary suffering on factory farms and in slaughterhouses.

Furthermore, we need to make sure that people who do change are able to maintain that change. While leafleting colleges across the country, activists very often meet people who tried to be vegetarian but failed because of poor health. When he leafleted regularly, Jack Norris heard this so frequently that it sometimes seemed he met more failed vegetarians than current vegetarians! Failed vegetarians tell everyone how awful they felt without meat, and how much better they feel as a meat eater again. Just one failed vegetarian can counter the efforts of many sincere advocates.

To do our best to prevent suffering, we must learn and present a complete, unbiased summary of the nutritional aspects of a meatless diet, including uncertainties and potential concerns. Vegan Outreach does this in our *Guide to Cruelty-Free Eating*, with a thorough article written by Jack, who, after meeting so many failed vegetarians, became a registered dietician. Providing this information not only leads people to trust that we are not just partisan propagandists, but it also creates healthy spokespeople for the animals!

If we want to be as effective as we possibly can be for the animals, it is absolutely essential that we stay focused on the animals. Our message is simple. We shouldn't try to answer every tangential argument. Whatever else is said cannot counter the fact that eating animals causes unnecessary suffering.

We must always stay focused on the animals. We are not the issue. Veganism is not the issue; it is only a tool for reducing suffering. Our purpose isn't to "win an argument with a meat eater." Our goal is to get people to open their hearts and minds to the animals' plight. We don't want to argue, we want to communicate: Buying meat, eggs, and dairy causes unnecessary suffering. We can each choose not to cause this suffering.

REASON FOR OPTIMISM

I understand that focusing on preventing animals from being bred for factory farms isn't a particularly exciting or inspiring prescription, especially compared to the pull of concrete campaigns, the plight of individual animals, or the immediacy of the latest tragedy. But if we take suffering seriously, we need to maximize our impact, rather than focus on the high profile.

I also know that this work can seem overwhelming and too slow. But recognize that our grassroots advocacy efforts are creating more vegetarians every day, leading to more vegetarian products arriving on the market every month. Having convenient vegetarian options is vital, as it makes it easier for new people to try and stick with a compassionate diet. As more people buy faux meats and other vegetarian products, competition will continue to increase the supply and varieties, improving quality and driving down prices. This cycle of increasing numbers of vegetarians and the increasing convenience of vegetarian eating creates a feedback loop that accelerates progress.

If we choose to focus our scarce resources on expanding this advocacy, the growth of vegetarianism will accelerate to a tipping point, where vegetarianism and opposition to factory farms become the "norm" among influential groups. Legislation, as it usually does, will continue to follow evolving public opinion, and we'll see more of animal agriculture's worst practices outlawed and abolished. Corporate practices will also continue to adjust to the demands from an increasingly aware market.

Economic forces will also drive change, because it is more economical to eat plant foods directly, rather than feeding plants to animals and then eating some of the animals' flesh. Of course, people aren't going to substitute tofu for meat; but that's not the choice they'll be making. Food science has already advanced such that the best vegetarian meats are already able to satisfy even hardcore carnivores. The faster the growth in the number of people choosing vegetarian, the faster vegetarian products will improve in taste, become cheaper, and be found in more places. Our challenge now is to expand the vegetarian market by explaining to more meat eaters the reasons for choosing meatless meals, while exposing them to new—though similar—products. The more rapidly we do this, the sooner cruelty-free eating will be widespread.

Despite all the current horror and suffering, if we take the long view—and are willing to commit to the work that needs to be done—we should be optimistic. If we take suffering seriously and are committed to optimal advocacy, we can each create real, fundamental change. This change will not come by revolution, but through person-by-person outreach progressing hand in hand with advances in technology, leading slowly but inexorably toward a new norm that, to most people, will hardly seem different. But an unfathomable amount of suffering will be prevented.

It is up to us to make this happen. I know that this can seem like unrewarding work, and the scale can appear intimidating. I know that the easiest thing would be to simply continue on as before, focused on the short term and high profile.

But we can be the leaders who fundamentally change society. We can each be extraordinary! The choice is ours, today and every day.

The Power of One

Vic Sjodin

2013

Growing up, I always liked dogs and zoos, and naturally considered myself an animal lover even though I was no friend to the innocent in my daily actions. There were moments when eating when I thought the dismembered parts—sinews, muscles, tendons in chicken legs, bloody steaks—were gross. But I just tried not to think about it. Chew and get it down the gullet. It was pretty easy when you didn't think about it.

When I was sixteen, I saw my mother, compassionate in all aspects of life, have her compassion evaporate as she entered the kitchen and put the water in the large pot to an ominous boil. Out of a brown paper bag came the condemned, hands manacled with elastic bands. I remember with horror when my mom shoved Sebastian into the boiling pot. The lobster tried to crawl out, and, as he was boiled alive, he let out a high-pitched scream unforgettable to me in its loudness and duration. While the others ate Sebastian, I felt sick. Still, I was weak and insecure, and I acclimated myself to what society expected. I ate animals, didn't think about them, and went on with my life being "normal."

Five years later, my consciousness was slowly awakened from a deep and prolonged slumber. While at Hofstra University, I was handed Vegan Outreach's *Why Vegan?* booklet. I scanned the booklet quickly and went to class. A few days later, I read the entire booklet, and it dawned on me before I was finished, "I have to go vegan." I loved burgers, pizza, cheese . . . *mmmm*. . . . I thought my palate would shrink. Initially it did, until it began a never-ending expansion.

My evolution was not overnight, though, and my will power was quite bendable; more like spaghetti than iron. Shamefully slowly, I started to cut back on animal products and within three years called myself a vegetarian, but I would still have Burger King Whoppers and pepperoni pizza every few weeks. In reality, I was a pizzaterian; I lived off pizza and had cheese on everything. Only two years later did I get close to true "vegan" (but even then I would still have cheese draped on hoagies once a week or so).

Deep within, I felt guilty for all the animals I had harmed by eating them, and I wanted their suffering to be known and to stop, so I volunteered and handed out Vegan Outreach's booklets at West Chester University in Pennsylvania. I wish I could say it was a good experience. It was not. I felt shy and very uncomfortable. It was freezing, the take rate was low, I was not standing in a good spot, and I felt super awkward and apprehensive. Afterward, I swore to myself "I will *never* do that again." I hated my whole time out there.

Yet, somehow I forced myself to do it again, and my apprehension embarrassed me. I felt like a coward. I told myself, "It really is no big deal, dude. Animals are going through horrors, and you're afraid to offer someone some information? Don't be a coward; this is the least you can do. Even if you feel uncomfortable, you are not in a crate and no one is going to kill you. Toughen up." So I forced myself to go out there, although there was a lot of inertia to overcome. Over time, there was less nausea and apprehension, and the deep-down awkward feeling dissipated faster and faster each day of leafleting.

Unfortunately, the animals are not going to free themselves. Justice needs us. The animals have not won the cosmic lottery like we have: being born human in a rich country and in a time of relative peace with all the freedoms that entails. We're not pigs in a cage, chickens hanging upside down entering the slaughterhouse.

I felt a deep connection to others and a responsibility to use my freedoms and privileges to free and help others. I felt soul-sick and listless when my days were used chasing dollars and endless pleasures. That did not equal happiness. I wanted purpose, and what could be more meaningful than living for a cause?

And that's how that one booklet changed the course of my life. That's how that one booklet was the catalyst for the booklet recipient to drive around North America for over six years, in a rusty old Buick, living without a permanent residence and handing booklets to over 700,000 new booklet recipients at over 500 schools in three countries. That, and give many talks and presentations, do a media tour, help ballot initiatives, midwife dozens of others to activism, make many new friends, and share innumerable laughs. It has been such an adventure. As a youth, I could never have dreamed the simple act of getting up early, driving, hitting the pavement, and handing people paper would take me to so many places, provide so many experiences, bring so many beautiful people into my life, and affect so many to adopt a compassionate life and start new ripples in their circles.

I have tried my best to be a voice for the oppressed and the innocent—to do my small part to make a compassionate life replace the callous and outdated "normal" of eating animals. I thank the universe for that seed—the booklet that altered the course of my life and started the slow transition to initially reducing meat consumption, then pizzaterianism, and eventually veganism. And that finally led to the fruit of activism, and thereby a far richer life of purpose and consciousness: an ethical and connected, happy, adventurous, and meaningful life.

It makes me happy to see that Vegan Outreach's *Why Vegan?* booklet from 2002 is still alive, rippling out and echoing in its impact on others. Our actions are eternal and contagious, and they affect the universe forever and ever. To those who produced, paid for, and handed me that sacred gift of awareness, know your actions are alive and still affecting more and more people from that one simple act. Thank you.

Is Being a Vegetarian Important?

Talk in Los Angeles, 2008

Have you ever been in so much pain that you thought you were going to die?

Have you ever suffered so much that you wanted to die?

Every year, hundreds of millions of individuals in the United States do suffer to death. Slowly. Excruciatingly.

Egg-laying hens packed in tiny wire cages, unable to move because of how crowded they are, can have their wings or necks get stuck in the wires, keeping them from getting to food or water.

Pigs, transported hundreds and hundreds of miles in all weather in open trucks without food or water, can freeze to death.

Chickens raised for meat, bred to grow so large so fast, can have their legs break under their own weight, leaving them incapacitated and unable to get food.

Vegan Outreach leafleter Wayne described watching a downed dairy cow's last few moments:

An hour before I was planning to leaflet, a friend of mine called and said that he had spotted a stalled transport truck with a downed dairy cow inside.

I arrived to witness a grisly scene. The poor girl was collapsed on the ground inside the truck, in a three-inch-deep cesspool of feces and urine. You could see her wide, terrified eyes staring into nothingness, her entire body quivering ever so slightly. But she was making no sounds. The other cows had trampled her broken body; she had bloody wounds and bright red lesions that were clearly visible through the filth. Her udder was swollen to many times its normal size. We noticed a ghastly sliver of flesh on a gate mechanism above her. (It was later suggested to us that this might have been her tongue. Cows tend to lick the sides of the truck in search of moisture, but when it's a frozen mechanized gate, that desperate attempt can have tragic consequences.)

Our poor friend died that day, on the filthy floor of a bloody transport truck. We witnessed her body go cold and her eyes stop moving. Her entire life had been enslaved and twisted by violence and prejudice.

Words cannot express the horrifying conditions that bring about these slow, agonizing deaths: how the animals are bred, how they "live" on factory farms, and, for those who survive the brutal system, how they are butchered in industrial slaughterhouses. No verbal or even video description can begin to capture it. Even visiting these confinement warehouses and slaughterhouses can't begin to convey what it is like to live one's entire life there, to be callously killed in the end.

It is enough to know that modern agribusiness is so inherently brutal that it will kill off, pre-slaughterhouse, hundreds of millions of animals through slow, agonizing means, simply as a cost of doing business. This is a system of cruelty so vast, so intense, that it really is beyond comprehension. Michael Pollan wrote the following in the *New York Times*:

> More than any other institution, the American industrial animal farm offers a nightmarish glimpse of what capitalism can look like in the absence of moral or regulatory constraint. Here in these places life itself is redefined—as protein production—and with it suffering. That venerable word becomes "stress," an economic problem in search of a cost-effective solution, like tail-docking or beak-clipping. Our own worst nightmare such a place may well be; it is also real life for the billions of animals unlucky enough to have been born beneath these grim steel roofs, into the brief, pitiless life of a "production unit."[1]

This is the system we endorse and support when we purchase its products. Consuming flesh foods from modern agribusiness not only pays others to exploit and butcher fellow feeling beings; it not only affirms the view of animals as unconsidered cogs in the machine of

1 Michael Pollan, "An Animal's Place," *New York Times*, November 10, 2002.

profit; but our purchases are what give agribusiness the resources needed to brutalize more individuals.

This is enough to compel me to be a vegetarian, to make a daily, public statement against the breathtaking viciousness behind meat, eggs, and dairy.

For me, being a vegetarian is not the conclusion of an impartial set of utilitarian calculations, nor the endorsement of "animal rights." Rather, being a vegetarian is a statement about the person I want to be: that I could not live with myself if I were to be a part of such unwatchable cruelty to animals. The phrase is, How could I look at myself in the mirror? And that is literally how it happened for me—looking in the mirror and realizing I couldn't consider myself a "good person" if I continued to pay others to brutalize animals so I could eat them.

But of course, not everyone makes this choice. With factory farms concealed and society structured around eating faceless, disembodied meat, we can easily refuse to take a stand and set ourselves apart. And if confronted with the hidden realities of modern agribusiness, we can seek out the "less bad" and call it good.

Michael Pollan, quoted earlier, not only isn't a vegetarian, he actively mocks the "moral certainty" of vegetarians. He fabricates fantastic rationalizations to continue eating animals. For example, he says that thinking in terms of individual animals is human-centric, and that we need to think in terms of species' interests. Of course, this is exactly backward. "Species" is a human construct, an abstraction that inherently can't have interests. Only individuals have the capacity to experience pleasure or suffer pain and thus have interests. That we should eat the flesh of our fellows to advance the "interests" of a species is so absurd, such a complete inversion of reality, it is truly stunning that a seemingly intelligent person would be willing to spout such ridiculous nonsense. Pollan is the perfect example of Cleveland Amory's observation that people have an infinite capacity to rationalize, especially when it comes to something they want to eat.

(This may seem an unnecessarily harsh condemnation of a man who at least is willing to write about factory farms. But Pollan not only mocks vegetarians via laughable straw man arguments, he even endorses the brutal act of force-feeding geese to create foie gras! This level of repulsive rationalization should be exposed for what it is.)

Pollan's unwillingness to honestly consider vegetarianism, combined with his firsthand experience of "our own worst nightmare," leads to his rationalizing capacity to praise "happy meat" from "humane" farms. Having had the time and resources to investigate the various farms available, the pinnacle of Pollan's praise is Polyface Farm, where "animals can be animals," living, according to Pollan, true to their nature.

So what is Polyface like? Rabbits on the farm are kept in small suspended-wire cages. Chickens are crowded into mobile-wire cages, confined without the ability to nest or the space to establish a pecking order. Pigs and cattle are shipped year-round in open trucks to conventional slaughterhouses. Seventy-two hours before their slaughter, birds are crated with seven other birds. After three days without food, they are grabbed by the feet, upended in metal cones, and, without any stunning, have their throats slit.

This is the system Pollan proclaims praiseworthy. While mocking vegetarians, he argues that we should ethically and financially endorse Polyface's view and treatment of animals.

But really, how can we expect better? In the end, Polyface's view is the same as Tyson's: These individual animals are, ultimately, just meat to be sold for a profit. It is logically and emotionally impossible for there to be any real respect, any true, fundamental concern for the interests of these individuals, when these living, breathing animals exist only to be butchered and consumed. If we insist that we must consume actual animal flesh instead of a vegetarian option, it is naïve, at best, to believe that any system will really take good care of the animals we pay them to slaughter.

If you say an individual is, fundamentally, just meat, they will be treated as such.

In the end, it really is a question of what kind of person we choose to be. Do we oppose cruelty or support slaughter? Do we make our own decisions or do we rationalize what we're used to doing?

I believe there are more important things in life than accepting the status quo, following the norms of society, and taking the easiest path.

Furthermore, choosing the road less traveled does not require denial and deprivation. Making our lives a part of something larger—opposing cruelty in our choices and working for justice—expands our life's narrative, enriches our existence, and allows for real meaning and lasting happiness. Choosing to be a vegetarian makes a public, powerful, ethical statement—not just about the suffering of animals, but about the strength of our character.

I ask you to consider one more thing: The average American consumes a few dozen land animals every year. By choosing to be a vegetarian, you will accomplish a great deal of good over the course of your life. You will spare many hundreds of animals from the malicious maws of modern agribusiness.

But get this: Tomorrow, you could accomplish much more, in just one hour!

This may sound like an infomercial scam, but it is true. For every person you convince to go vegetarian, you double the impact of your life's choices. So, if tomorrow you hand out sixty booklets to new people, and just one person decides to go vegetarian, you will have saved, in only one hour, just as many animals as you will save with every single choice you make over the rest of your life.

In other words, if we agree that being a vegetarian is important, then we must also recognize that being an effective advocate for the animals is many, many times more important. Efficient outreach has truly enormous potential: If you think compound interest is a good deal, effective vegetarian advocacy allows for exponential returns!

In his book, *Meat Market*, Erik Marcus writes:

When I was a teenager, my greatest ambition was to one day be a millionaire. [Later] I adapted the millionaire concept for purposes of activism. . . . I wanted to [keep] a million animals out of slaughterhouses. . . . But is it realistic to think that a typical

person could keep a million animals from slaughter?
Absolutely! . . . At two thousand [land] animals saved
per new vegetarian, this means that during your life,
if you convince five hundred young people to become
vegetarian, a million animals will be saved.

With a reasonable level of investment, each one of us
can do this. You don't need to start a group. You don't
need to pass a law. You just need to make the choice
to join with the others who are working for something
bigger than just themselves. We can provide you with
lessons from decades of experience and all the tools you
need. Vegan Outreach exists to help everyone and anyone, in every situation, to be the most effective advocate
possible for the animals—for a world not just a bit less
bad, but for a fundamentally better world.

Leaflets don't print themselves, however. Vegan Outreach is dependent upon the financial support of those
who recognize the importance of effective advocacy.
There are many demands on our limited time and money,
and we must choose to invest our scarce resources to do
the most good. Working to expose and end the hidden
horrors of factory farms is, we believe, the best possible
investment. Every new vegetarian pays dividends every
year, in terms of their food choices and the example they
set for others.

In 2007, Vegan Outreach distributed 1.8 million
booklets—56 percent more than in 2006. This was only
possible because, from fiscal year 2006 to 2007, contri-
butions to Vegan Outreach also rose 56 percent. Exactly
56 percent!

It is simple: A donation today will lead to more booklets to more people tomorrow, which will lead to new vegetarians and myriad animals spared this year, and every year!

In the end, in our hearts, we know that regardless of what we think of ourselves our actions reveal the person we really are. We can, like most, mindlessly accept the current default, follow the crowd, and take whatever we can.

Or we can actively author our lives, determining for ourselves what is important. We can live with a larger purpose, dedicated to a better world for all.

Quoting Myself

The Magic of Compounding Change

from *The Animal Activist's Handbook* by Matt Ball
and Bruce Friedrich

2009

Imagine that there are just 50,000 vegetarians
right now (there are actually millions) and that each
of these 50,000 convinces just one person to stop eating meat over the next five years. Imagine that those
100,000 convince just one person in the five years after
that, and that those 200,000, etc. In fewer than seventy
years, we have a vegetarian America, even accounting
for population growth. Most of us will do better than
influence one person every five years—some of us will be
able to open the hearts and minds of hundreds of people
every year. The harder we work, the faster we achieve
that vegetarian America we're striving toward.

Work Smarter, Not Harder

Talk in San Francisco, 2002

*This was written when Vegan Outreach distributed about
half a million booklets in 2002. Four years later, in 2006,
we distributed over a million booklets for the first time.
Since then, the number of animals killed in the United States
has steadily declined, even as the human population has
grown.*

To begin, I would like to list the specific facts on
which I base the rest of what I have to say:

- As revealed in the research of Dr. Donna
  Maurer, the percentage of the population who
  are true vegetarians in the United States has
  not changed significantly in decades.
- The average number of animals eaten per person each year in the United States is at or near
  its all-time high.
- The number of farmed animals killed in the
  United States increases by hundreds of millions
  each year. In 2002, nearly twice as many will be
  raised and slaughtered in this country as in 1980.

To me, these facts raise hard questions. The most obvious is, Why are things getting so much worse?

Since 1980, immense amounts of time and resources have been invested in working for the animals. There are many individuals who are extremely passionate about the issues, absolutely convinced that they are right, and totally committed to action.

And yet all these efforts have been a relative failure. Knowing that more and more animals continue to suffer, I feel compelled to question the premises of our work.

I don't think the answer is that we simply have to work harder. Having been an activist for more than a decade, I don't see any evidence to indicate that our current approach is lacking only in effort. I think that what is lacking, at least in part, is an elementary analysis, a fundamental grasp of goals and what it will take to achieve them.

No, I don't think we need to work harder. I think we need to work smarter. To do so, we must discard our assumptions and find a basis for our work, a first principle on which to first focus. We need to build a ground-up approach based on a solid foundation. We need to understand the "what" before addressing "how."

ASSUMPTIONS

Most of us have been taught that ethics is about justice and fairness, rights and freedom. However, from a universal perspective, it seems clear that "rights" and "justice" are not fundamental.

One way to see this is to ask, "Why?" Instead of, "What do we want?" ask, "Why do we want it?" Doing so shows that justice, fairness, and rights are all abstractions, relevant only as they affect suffering. We don't want rights as an end in themselves; we want them to prevent suffering. And we don't want to prevent suffering for any more fundamental reason: suffering is fundamental, irreducible. In a universal sense (which is the only means by which ethics can work) everything is irrelevant except in how it affects suffering. As Peter Singer writes in *How Are We to Live?*:

> The perspective on ourselves that we get when we take the point of view of the universe yields as much objectivity as we need if we are to find a cause that is worthwhile in a way that is independent of our own desires. The most obvious such cause is the reduction of pain and suffering, wherever it is to be found. This may not be the only rationally grounded value, but it is the most immediate, pressing, and universally agreed upon one. We know from our experience that when pain and suffering are acute, all other values recede into the background. If we take the point of view of the universe, we can recognize the urgency of doing something about the pain and suffering of others, before we even consider promoting (for their own sake rather than as a means to reducing pain and suffering) other possible values like beauty, knowledge, autonomy, or happiness (232).

Ultimately, the bottom line is this: Reduce suffering. Everything has to answer to this. I can't emphasize this enough: The only thing that matters is to reduce suffering. If you accept this as the *what*, the next question is, *how?* At this time, in this country, we choose to promote veganism. However, veganism is not an end in and of itself. We don't promote veganism because "veganism is good." Veganism is merely a tool to reduce suffering. Promoting veganism is promoting universal compassion and mercy. Promoting veganism is stating opposition to suffering.

DEFENSE OF DOGMA

And yet, many people get caught up in (their version of) veganism itself. They ask, "Is it vegan?" rather than "Does it reduce suffering?" They focus on defending a certain (and yet ultimately arbitrary) definition of "vegan" from those who would "corrupt" it. To them, defending a word is more important than actually preventing exploitation. Purity and consistency are more important than results.

Furthermore, many vegans lose all skepticism and sense of perspective. They believe anything remotely pro-vegan, or even slightly anti-meat. Health studies either show a vegan diet is the best or else the researchers are condemned as anti-vegan mercenaries. Veganism will cure anything and any speck of animal product is deadly poison. Any counterevidence is omitted; unknowns are dismissed; uncertainty is disregarded; gray areas are ignored.

Yet the world is gray and unclear.

OPEN QUESTIONS

When one replaces the question, "Is it vegan?" with "Does it reduce suffering?" the answers are not always clear. Here are just a few examples:

- What is the best way to spend money? For example, should we pay more for organic products, or save money and put it toward activism?
- What is the best way to earn money? Should we work for an animal-protection group, or try to maximize income to fund activism? Or should we work in a different field that could lead to a major payoff, such as perfecting the process for a cheaper meat substitute? Or growing animal-free meat?
- What about legislative reform, such as those enacted in the European Union? Or corporate reform, such as those brought about from the outside (the PETA/McDonald's agreement) or the inside (Burger King's BK Veggie Burger)? Or industry reform from the inside?

In terms of activism, there are even more questions: Is it best to promote veganism or vegetarianism, assuming more people will respond to the latter? Or should we attempt to address the absolutely worst areas by focusing on pigs, poultry, and eggs?

Even if one decides that, given the distribution of efforts throughout society today, promoting veganism is the best approach, questions remain. For example, what is the best use of our limited time and resources? Leafleting? Building a FaunaVision van with a video screen or Faunette (a small portable video screen)?[1] Seeking to get stories in the media?

---

1 The Faunette was pioneered by Eddie Lama and the focus of the documentary film *The Witness*, directed by Jenny Stein and produced by James LaVeck.

After many years, I have no clear answers to these (or other) questions. In fact, I don't even know how to go about approaching many of them, given the variables and uncertainties. However, I believe the best strategy is to be honest about the unknowns. I don't know how anyone can believe they have all the answers, and I think that many people are distrustful of those who present themselves as omniscient. I think it is relatively easy for most to dismiss others trying to "convert" them to a rule-based dogma or religion. But if issues are presented as fundamentally about trying to prevent suffering, it is harder for people to ignore.

WHY CARE?

Given the vastness of the cruelties of the world and the lack of clear answers to *How?*, it is understandable to fall back to asking, *Why?* Specifically, why should we care about reducing suffering?

Obviously, it is not only possible, but common, to live with concern only for ourselves, and perhaps a select few around us. The question then becomes, Is living a life of self-interest the most fulfilling life we can expect?

Without reference to a specific religious (or even philosophical) doctrine, there may appear to be no basis by which to judge ways of living. A materialistic life is often thought of as the external embodiment of the pursuit of pleasure, with pleasure being the ultimate "meaning" that life can have. With this in mind and a general understanding of our evolutionary heritage, one can better grasp the reasons why humans often attempt to derive their life's meaning from the pursuit of material goods.

Throughout the great majority of evolutionary history, those individuals who pursued and obtained the most (e.g., food and other signs of "wealth") survived and reproduced the most. This connection between having things and the continuation of one's genes was not conscious, but rather was manifested in the individual's drives and desires, a discontent with the status quo, and an envy of those with more.

These innate desires do not disappear once one has "enough" (when an individual is no longer in competition with others for limited resources or breeding rights). In fact, it would appear that in many, if not all, cases, nothing satisfies the drive for accumulating more. There is always more to have, there are always those better off to pursue. In other words, materialism is the embodiment of the pursuit of happiness, but it is ultimately incapable of arriving at happiness. More accurately, materialism is the attempt to satiate our insatiable evolutionary desires.

If taking more cannot lead to meaning and happiness, one alternative is creating something, giving something. That is, making an impact with our limited time, having our life be one of positive construction. Our existence can be a monument to something beyond our transient physical self: a better world.

Working together, working for something lasting, bigger than our individual self, can make life meaningful. Revisiting the myth of Sisyphus, condemned to roll a rock up a hill for eternity, Professor Singer argues that this ultimate torture can be made meaningful if Sisyphus is allowed to push different rocks up the hill and use them to construct a lasting monument. He also writes:

> We have to take the first step. We must reinstate the idea of living an ethical life as a realistic and viable alternative to the present dominance of materialist self-interest.
>
> Anyone can become part of the critical mass that offers us a chance of improving the world before it is too late. One thing is certain: you will find plenty of worthwhile things to do. You will not be bored or lack fulfillment in your life.
>
> Most important of all, you will know that you have not lived and died for nothing, because you will have become part of the great tradition of those who have responded to the amount of pain and suffering in the universe by trying to make the world a better place (235).

REASON FOR OPTIMISM?

Some might contend that this sounds good, but the situation is ultimately hopeless. Thus, it is a waste of time to bother with the fantasy of a "better world." I don't think this is true. Anyone interested in creating a fundamental change for the future is advised to take the long view—at least longer than the next year, or even decade. While it is frustrating how slow (or even negative) progress has been during the career of current activists, the rate of change among humanity has been unprecedented in the past century. Bruce Friedrich points out the following:

- 1633: Galileo is tried for the crime of heresy for proposing Earth is not the center of the physical universe.
- 1865: The 13th amendment outlawing slavery is passed in the United States.
- 1900: No country allowed all adult citizens to vote; now, more than 150 do.

The acceleration of change in human civilization is reason for a great deal of optimism. We have the great and singular opportunity to make the magazine *The Economist's* August 19, 1995, prediction (in an article entitled "What Humans Owe to Animals") come true: "Historically, man has expanded the reach of his ethical calculations, as ignorance and want have receded, first beyond family and tribe, later beyond religion, race, and nation. To bring other species more fully into the range of these decisions may seem unthinkable to moderate opinion now. One day, decades or centuries hence, it may seem no more than 'civilized' behavior requires."

Difficulty Does Not Equal Effectiveness

Dawn Ratcliffe

2010

Since becoming vegan in 1995, I have handed a Vegan Outreach booklet to over 170,000 individuals. Although I started using VO literature early on in my activism, I still felt that leafleting by itself wasn't as effective as protesting every weekend. I couldn't have been more wrong, especially when I looked at the amount of time I spent organizing protests, calling activists to attend the protests, making signs, etc. Maybe I felt that since I had invested so much time and effort, protesting had to be more effective than simply handing out leaflets for an hour or two. Thank goodness that Vegan Outreach continues to steer activists in the right direction!

Lincoln and the First Step

2013

My wife Anne Green and I finally watched the movie *Lincoln*, directed by Steven Spielberg, and we found it amazingly relevant. The hero is clearly Thaddeus Stevens (played by Tommy Lee Jones). More than anyone, he had reason to preach "no compromise" on equality, demand full abolition of any and all discrimination, and insist on nothing less than full and total rights immediately. He clearly would have been justified in raging with hatred at the venomous racists in Congress. (Even a century and a half later, knowing that history vindicates Thaddeus, it is difficult not to be appalled and outraged when watching a reenactment of this long-past debate.)

Yet Rep. Stevens didn't give in to his understandable anger. Instead of being "true to himself"—justified, righteous, and on the losing side—he chose possible progress over personal purity, incremental advance over impotent anger.

Progress over purity is VO's hard-won mantra. I wish one of us had summarized it as well as Jonathan Safran Foer, who, in his interview with Vegan.com's Erik Marcus, explained the two motivations for his book, *Eating Animals*: to be useful, not thorough; and to get new people to consider taking the first step, rather than demanding the last.

I was reminded of this on Facebook recently. Our friends at Compassion Over Killing have VegWeek, a positive, inviting, nonintimidating way to get new people interested in taking the first step. But in a FB post promoting VegWeek, too many judgers came out of the woodwork: "When you say 'veg,' you had better mean vegan!!" "Why just a week?? Be vegan forever!"

Of course, we all want our views and convictions to be validated, especially when currently held by only a minority. But the question is, Do we seek to justify our views/glorify ourselves, or do we want to get as many people as possible to take the first step for the animals? We may, like Thaddeus Stevens, burn with righteous anger, but we can also recognize that to make real progress to reduce real suffering, we need to get past our fury and embrace effective, thoughtful, focused advocacy.

If we really care about the animals first and foremost, we can abolish our personal desires and demands, and focus on making real, practical progress for the animals who are suffering to death every day. To do so requires opening the hearts and minds of others. This isn't done by anger and hatred, but by compassion and understanding.

Politics, Personal Conduct, and the Vegan Police

The Vegan Outreach Perspective

This piece originally appeared in Animal People, *October 2012.*

Having been prompted to do some broader thinking about the status of animal advocacy in the past year—including contrasting the recent AR2012 conference in Washington, DC with past AR conferences—I currently have a somewhat different perspective on the vegan police/absolutists, compared to my concerns when we were starting Vegan Outreach in the 1990s.

As the *Animal People* cofounders,[1] and longtime readers will remember, when Jack Norris, Anne Green, and I started working together more than twenty years ago, there was almost no strategic farmed animal advocacy or daily grassroots promotion of vegetarianism. More than 99 percent of animals who suffer harm

---

1 Animal People was cofounded by Kim Bartlett and Merritt Clifton. See www.animalpeoplenews.org.

from humans are killed to be eaten, but almost the only voices for them at the time were a relative handful of disconnected and usually isolated vegans. At the time, the vegan community was dominated—in volume if not numbers—by loud, judgmental, vegan-police types. There was no practical, pragmatic vision of how to create fundamental and growing change, and no dedication to, or even consideration of, optimizing advocacy. Most efforts went into defending and glorifying veganism. "How to win an argument with a meat eater" was the rallying cry—not "How to end factory farming and create a vegan society." This is why Vegan Outreach spent a fair amount of time addressing the vegan-police problem back then.

However, from Vegan Outreach's current perspective, those circumstances do not prevail any longer. Advocacy for farmed animals and promotion of vegetarian eating is a central concern—and often the sole focus—of organizations from the smallest local groups all the way up to the Humane Society of the United States.

The early years of Vegan Outreach were defined by trying to get people interested in strategic, constructive advocacy and outreach with the biggest possible impact for animals. Now, at the end of 2012, the most dynamic groups doing the most successful work in the United States are focused on farmed animal welfare and vegetarian promotion.

Vegan Outreach has literally thousands of otherwise unaffiliated volunteers who are active in exposing factory farms and promoting ethical eating—and doing so not in a dogmatic, arrogant manner, but in a pragmatic, psychologically informed fashion.

And we're just one of a large number of groups dedicated to optimal advocacy, focused on bringing about real, lasting change for the majority of people who are not vegans.

Here's another way to look at it: If you asked the average person on the street about vegans in 1995, that person would have mentioned their nephew's crazy misanthropic friend. When asked about vegans now, people think of Bill Clinton, Ellen DeGeneres, Jonathan Safran Foer, and the latest athlete to go vegan.

Of course, the screaming vegan police still exist—angry and basically impotent folks who focus not on cruelty to animals, but on hating vegans and vegetarians who have chosen to value pragmatism and results more than purity and exclusivity. There will always be those who draw self-worth from being apart from and superior to the rest, who want and need their exclusive vegan club.

Yet it is important to remember—and this is one of the most important lessons I've learned over the years—that those people have little impact in the real world, except in feeding a negative stereotype and wasting the time of practical, forward-looking advocates.

An analogy can be made with leafleting. We will sometimes come across a belligerent individual who wants to monopolize our time arguing. We can waste our time with this person, who will never change his mind and is only trying to undermine us. Or we can ignore that person and do the constructive and necessary work of reaching new people with the animals' message.

There are two practical consequences to this. The first is to recognize that angry, obsessive vegans are prevalent in society. Therefore, those of us focused on the animals must be the opposite of the stereotype that the angry and obsessive people create. For example, our longtime member Dan Kuzma tells this story:

> I talked to two Youngstown State English classes looking for topics for a paper. My talk was not what they expected. Many said the argument—reducing animal suffering—had no holes or flaws in it, essentially leaving them with no questions about why one should not eat animals. I kept on track the whole time using the "indisputable bottom line" argument for changing their diet. Essentially, my whole talk incorporated VO literature, which was very well received by the fifty students. When I polled them before class, two-thirds said they had had a "bad vegetarian experience"—i.e., conflict with a difficult vegetarian. I feel safe to say that the talks were good vegetarian experiences for the students. Many of the students decided to write about the issue and are rethinking the way that they eat.

The second can be summarized as follows: "Don't feed the trolls." Vegan Outreach is often contacted by people who say we must condemn group X, or rally our members in opposition to proposition Y or bill Z sponsored by group X. Or they attack us for not focusing on dairy, or want us to take a position on the latest controversy within the animal advocacy movement.

Instead of expending our limited time and resources on what history has shown to be endless and (at best) useless internecine debates, we simply wish everyone the best of luck in their efforts to help animals—and then we continue with the constructive, necessary work of exposing factory farms and promoting ethical eating to new people.

A Most Unlikely Advocate

Joe Espinosa

2013

In October of 1992, I was a senior in biology at the University of Illinois, walking into the Union to cash a check and buy a soda. In the Union foyer I took notice of a rather loud local berating a student who was tabling for a student organization. I stopped to watch and listen and discovered that the student was showing video footage of the way modern farming treats animals. The objector was a dairy farmer.

I was impressed with the calm and factual demeanor of the student and rather embarrassed for the dairy defender. Once the angry animal agriculturalist left, I scooted up to watch the video of how chickens and turkeys are raised, transported, and slaughtered. I let the student know that I, too, had a background in dairy farming, having learned dairy farming from my uncle in Wisconsin as a child, but I had no plans to berate him for presenting uncomfortable truths about our treatment of other animals.

Although I was in the College of Agriculture when I entered the university, during my first semester I had decided to change to pursue a degree in biology, as I was not really comfortable with the idea of spending my life harming animals. I had never seen the way modern farming treats birds, who, as it turns out, endure the most suffering of any of the traditionally farmed animals.

The student allowed me to absorb this view of modern farming, invited me to take the printed material that had more information and documentation, and also invited me to the weekly meetings of the student animal protection group, Students for Animal Rights. I read through the material I had taken, decided to go to the next meeting, and the next, and the next, but I missed the fourth meeting in an effort to turn away from the hard and ugly truth about the brutality we inflict on other animals.

That student—Matt Ball—called me to invite me back to the group the day after I missed the fourth meeting. I showed up to the next week's meeting to let the group know that I had not eaten meat in six days and did not think I could ever go back.

My work for animals had just begun.

As of December 2013, Joe Espinosa[1] has handed a Vegan Outreach booklet to more than 460,000 students and young people all across the Midwest, which puts him easily among the top-ten all-time VO leafleters. He has accomplished this while working a full-time job as a social worker in a methadone clinic. In 2008, Joe won the national Henry Spira Grassroots Activist Award.

---

1 See www.veganoutreach.org/enewsletter/espinosa.html.

Animals Matter

Interview with Fuente Vegana, January 2010

Many vegan advocates, including Vegan Outreach, say that going vegan or reducing our consumption of animal products will directly save lives. Is this really true? Don't subsidies artificially keep up the number of animals killed, even if demand drops?

Subsidies can distort market signals, but they can't eliminate them. Because of changes in what people buy, there was an increase in the number of animals killed for many years. Likewise, there has recently been a decline in the number of land animals killed for food in the United States in spite of continuing subsidies. (See also *Does Being a Vegetarian Really Save Animals?*[1])

Vegan Outreach focuses on leafleting to college students, and you estimate that about 1 to 3 percent of people who take a brochure will actually change their diet. Can we somehow increase this percentage by tar-

---

1 www.veganoutreach.org/articles/saveanimals.html.

geting different and maybe more open audiences with specific material?

There is a trade-off on cost and specificity. We could, for example, hand out full-color books that might have a higher change rate, but only afford to hand out a hundredth the number. Or we could hand out many more one-page black-and-white leaflets, but they wouldn't have the power to move people to make real change.

Everything is subject to a cost–benefit analysis. Vegan Outreach does, for example, have a music-specific cover for leafleting the Warped Tour in the summer, and we have both *Even If You Like Meat* and *Compassionate Choices* for leafleting. But we have to realize that there is no magic message that will move everyone. We have to reach those willing to change, and realize that no matter what tactic or message, this is currently only a fraction of people.

New figures show that about 2 percent of the US population eats a vegan diet (not counting honey). I assume this is the highest percentage anywhere in the world. Is this Vegan Outreach's work? How can other countries catch up?

I don't know if the United States is highest; the United Kingdom might have a higher percentage. I know Vegan Outreach's work is changing a lot of people,[2] and that this type of grassroots education is really important in increasing the number of people who choose a compassionate diet.

---

2 "Selected Recipient Feedback," Vegan Outreach: www.veganoutreach. org/feedback.html.

The United States may be able to provide a good example of the importance of changing advocacy focus. For many years, the focus here was on fur and vivisection, and the number of animals killed every year skyrocketed (land animals slaughtered went up by many, many billions). In the early 1990s, Vegan Outreach started arguing we should focus on the 99 percent of animals generally ignored—those butchered to be eaten. Now, vegetarianism is common and growing, and factory farms are widely condemned.

I think Vegan Outreach's Adopt a College program is the only one of its kind in the world. Do you have any tips for people who want to start something similar in their own countries? In many countries there are no free or cheap full-color brochures available, and people are afraid that spending a lot of money on printing leaflets and brochures could be just a waste of their money.

Of course, many activists are unhappy with the results they are currently getting, but uneasy about changing away from what other activists are doing. But there is a saying: If you want a different result, you have to try something different. So my first tip is to question the status quo and query what type of activism is considered the "norm." We should look at our options in terms of payoff per dollar spent and hour worked, rather than what is simplest, cheapest, and/or most common. We always need to be focused on the bottom line of reducing as much suffering as possible.

In my experience, most vegans are not "activists." Many maybe think that actively promoting veganism would be an exhausting sacrifice and that in the end it wouldn't make a difference. Could you please comment on this?

I would suggest they read, on our Web site, our blog, and our Facebook page, the experiences of activists and the lives being changed every day!

And just look at the numbers. The Vegetarian Resource Group's 2009 poll estimates 3.4 percent of the United States' adult population are real vegetarians. This is up from 2.3 percent in 2006. If you extrapolate to the population as a whole, this would indicate more than 3.5 million new vegetarians between polls.

If your main goal is to reduce animal-product consumption overall, why don't you use health and environmental arguments, like the "Meat Free Mondays" campaign? Wouldn't this be more effective? Don't most people go vegetarian for health reasons?

Our main goal isn't to reduce consumption; it is to lessen suffering. For many decades, groups and individuals thought they could trick people into making compassionate choices. But the "health argument" and various environmental arguments have led to many people switching from eating a few large animals to many smaller—and more intensively raised—animals, like chickens. This has led to a great deal more suffering.

We focus on the animals because they matter. If we are going to reduce the animals' suffering, we need people to recognize and consider their suffering. The ethical case for vegetarianism is simple, straightforward, and indisputable. Vegan Outreach member Dan Kuzma recently spoke to a college class and reported the following:

> My talk was not what they expected. Many said the argument—reducing animal suffering—had no holes or flaws in it, essentially leaving them with no questions about why one should not eat animals. Many of the students decided to write about the issue and are rethinking the way that they eat.

In your advocacy you usually don't mention the "basics of why vegan": that no matter how eggs are produced, there will be useless male chicks, and that no matter how dairy is produced, there will be forced pregnancies and male calves that cannot produce milk. Why do you leave this out?

Vegan Outreach's point isn't to justify our own views or catalog all cruelty. Rather, we want to create as much real change as possible in a society where eating an actual chicken leg is rarely even questioned. "Rights," "veganism," and other human constructs are irrelevant—all that matters is reducing as much suffering as possible.

Why do you not directly promote animal rights? Isn't this necessary to establish a permanent change in the way we relate to animals and also to avoid the suffering of animals in the future?

We are seeking to reach as many non-vegans as possible where they are in society as it actually is today. Very few people will go from eating meat to thinking in terms of animal rights. On the other hand, a large majority of people already oppose cruelty to animals, regardless of their personal philosophy or religion.

Again, our advocacy isn't about the last step; it is about the first step. As you know, people evolve over time, and if we can get them to take the first step, Vegan Outreach's *Guide to Cruelty-Free Eating* and our Web site provide tools to help them learn and take further steps. Similarly, societies change over time, and the optimal advocacy message will, in turn, change over time. But now, few people will change when exposed to a totally foreign philosophy, compared to those who will be moved when they see the hidden realities of modern agribusiness.

In my experience, promoting veganism often leads peo-ple to only go vegetarian. People choose their own steps and their own pace anyway. Why do you think it is nec-essary to tell people that opposing cruelty to animals is not an "all-or-nothing proposition"? I'm sure many vegans feel it is wrong to say that it is "OK" to "only eat less meat, eggs, or dairy."

It isn't our goal to document all cruelties and injustices in the world. We aren't out to say what is or isn't "OK." We're not about preaching or dictating morals. We don't seek to explain or justify our views or to celebrate veganism. Furthermore, opposing cruelty to animals simply isn't an "all-or-nothing proposition." No one is perfect; no vegan is pure. Everyone is causing suffering at some level, and no one is doing their absolute best to prevent/eliminate suffering.

Not only is it less effective to act like there is some ultimate answer or perfect diet, but it simply isn't true.

As you point out, people evolve over time. Our purpose is to start that change, not to present the most complete case for our current personal views. We're not the point: Maximum change for the animals is what matters. The key to this is recognizing that only meat eaters are in a position to save animals from the horrors of factory farms, so their mind-set and motivations are what matters.

Vegan Outreach activists have personally dealt with many millions of individuals in various situations, and they have consistently reported people who have had knee-jerk reactions to the word "vegan." For example, "Oh, I could never be vegan," or "I know a vegan, and they are a fanatic." Thus, they close themselves off to considering the message and making any change.

Bruce Friedrich has had personal interactions with literally thousands of individuals over the years. He recently wrote the following:

> I actually think that using the word "vegan" (other than perhaps with youth) may be counterproductive to helping animals, relative to using the word "vegetarian." As a species, we are given to seeing things as "all or nothing," and I can't tell you how many times I've

had discussions with people who write off making any changes because they believe they can't go vegan.

That's why I no longer wear my "Ask me why I'm vegan" shirts—I wear the vegetarian ones, and the conversations have gotten so much better! Where people used to be all about what vegan means and how hard it is to give up dairy (which saves 1/10 of an animal/year), now we talk about fish and chickens (saving many dozens of animals/year). I used to hear stories about dour and angry vegans; now I hear stories about daughters and cousins who are vegetarian.

This is anecdotal, of course, but it's not theoretical—this is real-world and overwhelming! I have far, far more people respond to my shirt now and approach me to ask questions. Before, I generally talked about what vegan means and the evils of dairy (still good, of course, but not nearly as valuable in helping animals). Now, I often have people tell me on the basis of one conversation that they will go vegetarian.

My long experience shows the word *vegan* scares many people, but the word *vegetarian* interests them (we also see this overwhelmingly when leafleting—people want vegetarian information far more than vegan information). Ironically, I'll bet we get far fewer vegans by using the word *vegan*, since many vegetarians do go vegan once they see how easy it is and start down the path of compassionate eating.[3]

---

3 Personal correspondence, January 10, 2010.

Vegan Outreach is all about getting results. Not about theory, or to say what is wrong, or which words philosophers prefer, but what experience shows and what psychologists and marketers have found works. The bottom line is simple: More change, fewer animals suffering.

Messaging for Maximum Change

Kenny Torrella

2010

I read [Bruce's insight regarding "vegetarian" vs. "vegan"] a few weeks ago and have been experimenting with it lately. I think it's a small tip for activists that goes a long way.

For two and a half years, I had been telling people I was vegan if the subject came up. Now if people ask, I say I'm vegetarian, and it makes a world of difference. When I used to say I was vegan, people would immediately say some kind of variation of, "That's awesome, but I could never do that myself." Now when I say I'm vegetarian, people become more open and tell me about other vegetarians they know, vegetarian foods they've tried, how they've considered going vegetarian, or that they were vegetarian in the past and want to get back into it.

Whenever I met a vegetarian while leafleting, I used to say, "Have you considered veganism?" The situation would immediately turn a bit sour. For a split second they saw me as someone they had much in common with; after asking if they've considered veganism, they see me as someone telling them to do more—that their vegetarianism is not enough. Out of the number of vegetarians I had met and responded to like this, not a single one responded positively—none said, "Why yes, I have been considering veganism lately!" All of them said a variation of, "Well, veganism seems like a good thing, but it's just too much for me." No matter how much cajoling, they wouldn't budge. The funny thing about this is that when I was a vegetarian I was the same way toward vegans. This is something important to remember. I didn't go vegan because another vegan was telling me to, or even telling me about it. I did it on my own after thinking about it and researching it for several months.

Now, while leafleting I give words of encouragement to vegetarians I meet. I tell them how awesome it is that they're vegetarian, to keep it up. I say: "Aw, you're the best." I give them literature that has recipes and nutritional information (such as Vegan Outreach's *Guide to Cruelty-Free Eating*). This makes a huge difference! They feel encouraged to do more, rather than being told to. They may not feel as alone in their choice if they meet another "vegetarian" who is also an activist and is thanking them.

Although our initial reaction is to identify as a vegan or to convince vegetarians to go vegan, nine times out of ten it doesn't turn anyone on to veganism. It only makes them feel like they're being judged, as if their lifestyle choice to eschew all meat products was worth nothing.

I'm not saying this is a fool-proof guide to live by: Of course there are instances where it's important to say you're vegan. If a vegetarian wants more information about going vegan, then by all means, hand out vegan literature and share your experiences as a vegan.

Although I was at first skeptical of Friedrich's tip, I experimented with it and found it to be a much better approach toward turning more people on to a vegetarian lifestyle.

Book Summary— Switch: How to Change Things When Change Is Hard

With Anne Green

2010

As you know, Vegan Outreach is dedicated to creating as much real change as possible. To that end, we study widely (marketing, psychology, sociology). A book useful for people seeking to improve their activism is *Switch*. For those not in a position to read the whole thing (though it is a quick and anecdote-filled read), we'll try to hit on the key points as applicable to Vegan Outreach/animal advocacy.

The Heaths start with the analogy set out in *The Happiness Hypothesis* by Jonathan Haidt:

> Haidt says that our emotional side is an Elephant and our rational side is its Rider. Perched atop the Elephant, the Rider holds the reins and seems to be the leader. But the Rider's control is precarious because the Rider is so small

relative to the Elephant. Anytime the six-ton Elephant and the Rider disagree about which direction to go, the Rider is going to lose. He's completely overmatched (7).

In short, the Heaths' hypothesis is that to bring about change, we have to do the following: direct the Rider; motivate the Elephant; shape the Path. There are three subsections under each of these steps, and Vegan Outreach leafleters have experienced all of them.

A. DIRECT THE RIDER

1. *Follow the Bright Spots*

Instead of starting from scratch, look for points of common ground. In our case of advocating for the animals, don't assume an adversarial (or teaching) position. Rather, find common areas from which to build. Nearly everyone opposes cruelty to animals (and those who say they don't often do, once you get past the posturing). This is an incredibly powerful bright spot! Do they have or have they had a companion animal? Do they "not eat much meat"? Do they like Boca burgers, or know a vegetarian? Do they have a similar background to you?

You can even take what appears to be a negative and use it as a hook, as Vegan Outreach does with the title of our booklet, *Even If You Like Meat*.

Mikael wrote about an encounter he had while he was leafleting:

One woman stopped and said she loved meat. I told her I did, too, but when I examined my morals and values, they did not match up with my actions and therefore I stopped eating meat. I also suggested that she give up meat on Mon/Wed/Fri and see how that went. She seemed like she would totally give it a try.

2. Script the Critical Moves

"Don't think big picture; think in terms of specific behavior." In other words, don't say, "Go vegan!" No one changes from such an exhortation (see "Shrink the Change," below). Rather, give people specific steps they can take to start on the path of change: not eating chicken and pigs, avoiding all food from factory farms, not eating meat several days a week, etc.

Phil reports that after talking to two guys while he was leafleting, "They both still seemed a little unwilling to never eat meat again. I mentioned that even cutting down on meat lessens a lot of suffering. One got excited and said, 'I can do that!' They both walked away intently reading the leaflets."

3. Point to the Destination

"Change is easier when you know where you're going and why it's worth it." Again, don't talk in terms of big picture abstractions ("liberation," "sustainability," "environment"). Rather, stick to what speaks directly to the individual.

Nikki reports:

A professor invited me to address his seventy-plus student class. I gave a quick introduction and said, "Listen, even if you just cut animals out of three dinners per week, that would be a huge help for our animal friends. If you read this, please pass it on—the more people know, the quicker this insanity ends." I then asked who wanted to read a booklet. Not hearing a peep in the room, I stepped off the stage, looked up, and half their arms were raised!

B. MOTIVATE THE ELEPHANT

1. *Find the Feeling*

"Knowing something isn't enough to cause change. Make people feel something." Many vegans think a purely philosophical, statistics-filled, intellectual argument should be enough to cause people to change. But the Heaths point out this is absolutely not the case; the rational Rider actually has little control over the emotional Elephant.

This is obviously the key to Vegan Outreach's approach: Show people the hidden cruelty to animals. What people feel has to be a powerful enough feeling to overcome inertia, habits, etc.

Eileen summarized the comments from one leafleting outing this way:

"Oh man, this is the packet that made me vegetarian!"

"Aw, this is the booklet that made me go vegetarian last year!"

"I went vegetarian from this!"

"I like meat, but this is just so horrible!"

And here's some feedback from FR:

"I feel so good helping animals and have helped some of my friends go vegan. Thanks for inspiring me!"

2. Shrink the Change

"Break down the change until it no longer spooks the Elephant."

This is the key lesson from the book! Of course, it goes without saying that we want everyone to be vegan. We want this because we don't want any animals to suffer for "food." The key here isn't the "vegan" abstraction, but the animals' suffering—very real and concrete. The way to address this is not to trumpet veganism, but to get more and more people to eat fewer and fewer animals.

SQ:

While I appreciate [another group's] goals, their all-or-nothing tone always left me feeling guilty and discouraged. Vegan Outreach is the first vegan advocacy and information site that I've seen that makes me feel good about my recent decision to drop meat and fowl and explore new foods and cooking methods. Kudos for making a convincing case for veganism without making people feel selfish and evil if they don't get to 100 percent immediately!

3. Grow Your People

"Cultivate a sense of identity and instill the growth mind-set." In this chapter, the Heaths talk about how to capture people's preexisting inclinations (find the bright spot—opposition to cruelty to animals), and get them to start thinking that change really is possible. The way to make the possibility of change real is by getting them to make a small change. Then they think of themselves as someone who can change, not someone limited by habit, peer pressure, etc.

Jon:

> Last night, Hoss was talking about how creating change isn't always as simple as giving people facts. People have a tough time admitting their previous way of living was wrong. That is what I have always liked about the Vegan Outreach approach—it allows people the opportunity to make changes while still being able to save face. And then the changes lead to more changes; soon the originally held positions have also changed. It's actually quite subversive.
>
> I saw the results of this approach today at Rochester Institute of Technology. One young woman came up to tell me that, three years ago, she received an *Even If You Like Meat* on campus. She liked the idea of "you don't have to be perfect" and immediately cut her meat consumption to basically nothing. She told me that since receiving the booklet, she has consumed meat three times—an average of once per year. The "not all or nothing" proposition sold her and continues to keep her on board.
>
> Also, a faculty member told me a story about her coworker. She once got an *Even If You Like Meat* and tacked it to her bulletin board for whatever reason; she

continued to look at it, to make changes, and she is now vegetarian.

C. SHAPE THE PATH

1. Tweak the Environment

"When the situation changes, the behavior changes." Vegan Outreach can't directly alter people's environment, but we do take advantage of when people change their environment by going away to school.

Theo: "At Santa Clara University, a student mentioned that the booklets had been brought up in one of his classes, and for the most part the students agreed with what was said inside."

Aaron: "These booklets are becoming recognizable on campuses everywhere. Several students today knew exactly what it was before I handed it to them, and so many said that it is what prompted them to try vegetarian/vegan."

2. Build Habits

"When behavior is habitual, it's 'free'—it doesn't tax the Rider." Unless you can move everyone into a vegan household, it isn't going to be easy to build new habits. But combine this with "Shrink the Change" and you'll see the opportunity: Modify current habits slightly such that people can stay close to their current routine but still make a difference.

In other words, don't expect people to stop eating fast food and making what is convenient and switch over to a diet of slow-cooked, whole-food, organic, local, fat-free quinoa, amaranth, and bok choy, topped with nutritional yeast "cheese" and sprinkled with chia seeds. Rather, promote a diet that fits in with their current habits: quick microwaved Boca burgers and Amy's dinners, bean burritos, Tofurky sandwiches, Field Roast sausages, etc.

3. Rally the Herd

"Behavior is contagious. Help it spread." Being a positive, confident vegetarian example in public shows people it can be done, allows those interested to ask questions, and gives support to other vegetarians.

Nikki:

Leafleting at the beach was great today! Four teenage girls eagerly received their booklets:

Girl #1: "Ugh, I can't look at these pictures!"

Girl #2 (to me): "Are you vegetarian?"

Me: "Yes."

Girl #4: 'What do you eat?'

Me (while giving them *Guides*): "Everything other than our animal friends—easiest thing I've ever done!"

Girl #1: "That's it! Let's do it! I can't look at these pictures. . . . I need to go vegetarian. Seriously, let's do it! Now! Done."

Girls #2–4: "OK. OK. Done!"

Vic: "One girl at William Paterson today said she had been wanting to go veg, so she got a *Guide*. Another two girls who are roommates said they would go veg for a week, so they got a *Guide* and encouragement."

Yvonne: "A couple of girls who walked by said, 'Hey, I'll become a vegetarian if you do.' 'Yeah, let's!' One girl ran to her group and shouted, 'Guess what? I'm going to become a vegetarian!'"

"Shrink the Change" and "Shape the Path" indicate that the easier change is (i.e., the more vegetarians that are around and the more familiar vegetarian options that are available), the easier it is for people to start on the road of change. This approach also suggests that a campaign to get more cruelty-free options available on college campuses (and providing local information and social support) could have a very significant payoff.

"You're the Best Kind of Vegan."

Ellen Green (lifelong vegan)

2013

So a whole bunch of us went to Scripps College for dinner, and Louie was talking about what cooking she and her partner were planning to do during finals week for everyone. They wanted to make sure they had a vegan option available for me, so Naomi asked me if I have vegan sweetener. My response to this was basically, "What?" I had never heard of such a thing.

They said they just have honey and sugar, so I told them both were definitely fine, because my opinion is bee sentience is limited and any animal products involved in sugar are so low down on the suffering scale that I don't really care. (Anyway, insects are killed in the production of *everything*.) This led me to a brief explanation of the pie chart[1] of animals killed per year from the aver-

---

1 "Vegan Outreach's Focus, in One Graph," Vegan Outreach, June 22, 2013: http://whyveganoutreach.blogspot.com/2013/06/piegraph.html.

age American diet, and how dairy's not even a sliver. I closed with, "And it's about ninety-plus percent eggs and chicken, really."

Louie looked contemplative and said, ". . . I guess I really should give up eggs. But they're in so many good Thai dishes! I mean, I could give up omelets and scrambled eggs, but . . ."

To which I replied, "So don't give up eggs in Thai dishes, just give up the rest."

Louie looked up at me, apparently wildly impressed, and said, "I like you!"

I just told her, "I mean, I'd rather have you do something to help animals than do nothing, really."

Louie concluded: "You're not a jerky vegan. You're the best kind of vegan."

IV.
FOCUS

Animals, Not Arguments

2010

When I went vegan more than twenty years ago, a common theme was to "win an argument with a meat eater." Every topic was fair game, and every question or theory—no matter how tangential or absurd—was argued fanatically.

I fell into this trap too, believing and parroting the most outrageous claims about impotence, water usage, and other absurdities. It took me a long time to realize the point isn't to show how many claims I had memorized, or to glorify my veganism, or to "defeat" a meat eater. Rather, the bottom line is to help animals by helping more people make informed, compassionate choices.

Nonetheless, many dubious "pro-veg" claims continue to float around today, undermining effective advocacy for the animals. For example, some vegans feel the need to claim that veganism is "natural" (whatever that might mean). To this end, the vegan diet (as though there is a single vegan diet) has to be perfect in and of itself: no planning required, and no supplements. This leads to one of the most harmful fantasies: that we don't need to worry about particular nutrients, especially vitamin B_{12}.

Jack Norris has worked against this delusion for as long as Vegan Outreach has existed. But still, there are people more committed to dreams than reality, as evidenced by Jack's continual need to address the latest incarnation of this insidious myth.[1]

Of course, I understand the desire to believe that veganism is our natural diet (and would cure baldness, feed the hungry, bring world peace). But our goal isn't to show how awesome veganism is. What is important is saving animals. To do this requires an honest evaluation of reality, from the nutritional aspects of veganism to the psychology of how people can and do change.

Still, many activists think, "If one argument for vegetarianism is good, then ten are better, and a hundred are even better!" But this is actually the opposite of how human psychology works. An argument for significant change isn't strengthened by volume. Rather, any case for change is a chain—only as strong as its weakest link. Past a certain point, every additional argument offered to a non-vegetarian both dilutes and distracts from the strongest argument for making compassionate choices.

Instead of being left with the concrete, indisputable connection to cruelty, the case often presented leaves many meat eaters thinking the following:

- "Yeah, maybe I should get a chicken sandwich instead of that burger."

---

1 Jack Norris, "Vitamin B12: Are You Getting It?" VeganHealth.org: http://veganhealth.org/articles/vitaminb12.

- "What I eat isn't really going to impact someone starving in Africa."
- "What I eat isn't really going to affect global warming."
- "This reminds me of that story explaining how chicken is so much more environmentally friendly than beef."
- "Gawd, what a fanatic—like I'm gonna eat only unprocessed fruits and vegetables."
- "They think animals are more important than people!"

As we've said before, meat eaters are the only ones in a position to save animals in the future. We have to engage them in a realistic, constructive, and honest manner—not glorify ourselves or impress other vegans.

Of course, just as I appreciate the desire to believe veganism has magical powers, I realize that it can be hard to be vegan in this society. For example, I recently heard one woman's story of being harassed by people at work deliberately eating meat right in front of her, and sending crude anti-animal e-mails to her workgroup. I absolutely understand the desire to defend our personal veganism with an endless litany of arguments, so as to "win an argument with a meat eater." But again, defending ourselves/winning an argument is actually the opposite of how best to create real change for the animals in today's society. Any time we offer an argument that can be debated (caloric conversion ratios, water usage, mortality/specific disease rates, relative carbon footprints/nutrition quality), the animals lose.

Whenever I mention that we must stay focused on the indisputable bottom line of cruelty to animals, some folks reply: "But my Uncle Bubba doesn't care about animals! I have to appeal to his self-interest!" or "Suzy at Meetup said she went veg for health reasons, so it obviously works!"

It is hard to accept, but Uncle Bubba is ultimately irrelevant to our current work for the animals. He will be dead long, long before he could possibly become the impediment to a vegetarian society. Instead, our insistence on believing in and promoting the "magic" argument that "appeals to everyone" will, at best, lead Uncle Bubba to replace red meat with much smaller chickens and fishes, with the net result that his choices cause many, many more animals to suffer. Of course, this will also reinforce the idea that we should only do what we feel is in our best interest.

When I stopped eating animals, about five billion birds were killed in the United States each year. Now it is almost ten billion—all because of "self-interest." We advocates obsess over the fact that the "health argument" convinced raw foodist Suzy at Meetup, and we conveniently ignore our culpability for the near doubling of animals slaughtered for "healthy" food. It is simply wrong, on every level, to turn a blind eye to the huge increase in the number of animals suffering and the reason behind that horror: self-interest.

Let me emphasize again that I want to do whatever I can to reduce the number of animals suffering. I totally sympathize with the desire to find the perfect self-centered argument that will appeal to more people. But we can only help animals by being more interested in reality than our personal desires. How powerful an argument seems to us is utterly irrelevant. Only by working in the real world and convincing more non-vegetarians to make net positive change can we really help animals.

The facts are simple, stark, and indisputable:

1. At this time, there simply is no magic argument or combination of arguments that will convince everyone—or even a majority—to go vegan.
2. The health argument, as it is actually interpreted and acted on in the real world by non-vegetarians, has killed many, many more animals than it has spared.
3. Every additional argument we present to meat eaters gives them more distance between themselves and their real and immediate connection to the brutality on factory farms.

We must each ask ourselves this question: Will we work for the animals in the world as it is, or live in the feel-good vegan echo chamber?

Each of us can make a real, significant difference. But we can't afford to make my past mistakes again, or try to win an argument. Rather, we must focus on the animals.

Even if they were all valid, trying to use multiple arguments makes us less effective advocates with the people who might potentially make changes for the animals. Furthermore, many of these arguments can do active harm to the animals when their overall net impact is assessed. When we offer arguments that reinforce the idea that everyone should be motivated only by self-interest, we reinforce society's call for people to change from eating large animals to smaller animals. Therefore, we must always assess the total net impact of our advocacy on all animals—not just whether an argument sounds good to us or has worked for a few individuals we happen to know. Regardless of how a story, study, or claim sounds to us, if there is any chance it could lead non-vegetarians to eat more chickens and/or fish, we should not promote it.

Lesson Learned

Advocacy Can Hurt Animals

Why Vegan Outreach blog, February 2013

Let's say we have developed what we think is the most powerful pro-veg argument ever, and we present it to ten people. Incredibly, five of them stop eating animals; the others decide to "eat better"—following the mainstream suggestions of their doctor and friends by giving up red meat.

We might think, "50 percent conversion rate? That must be the way to go!" This is how I used to think. But after years, I finally learned to ask: How does this argument actually affect animals?

Every year, the average American eats twenty-three birds, a third of a pig, and a tenth of a cow.[1] It currently takes about 193 birds (chickens plus turkeys) to provide the same number of meals as one steer. It takes fifty-six birds to equal one pig.

So, before our presentation, the ten people consumed

---

1 Citations can be found at http://whyveganoutreach.blogspot. com/2013/02/lesson-learned-advocacy-can-hurt-animals.html.

a combined 234 land animals every year. After our presentation, the same ten—including the five who joined our vegetarian club—eat 296 land animals per year. This is because even though our argument convinced fully half of them to stop eating animals entirely, the others replaced their red meat intake with birds in order to eat more healthfully.

Moving from red meat to chicken is a well-documented fact. For example, "'If you look at dietary recommendations put forth by the US Department of Agriculture [and other health institutions[2]], they are to decrease red meat and substitute lean meat, poultry and fish,' says Daniel [a nutritional epidemiologist at the University of Texas MD Anderson Cancer Center]. 'We've seen in other data that people are gravitating toward poultry.'"[3]

Finally, the National Institutes of Health notes "the growing preference in the US for poultry, but not fish, as a replacement for red meat."[4]

There are contradictory studies on how much chicken is eaten by people who give up red meat entirely. But for people who reduce the amount of red meat they eat—the majority of people who change their diet for health rea-

---

2 "Cutting Red Meat—For a Longer Life," Harvard Health Publications, from Harvard Medical School, June 2012: http://bit.ly/1cThqW8:.

3 Eliza Barclay, "Why There's Less Red Meat on Many American Plates," National Public Radio, June 27, 2012: http://n.pr/1cThghl.

4 Carrie R. Daniel, Amanda J. Cross, Corinna Koebnick, and Rashmi Sinha, "Trends in Meat Consumption in the United States," NIHPA, November 12, 2010: www.ncbi.nlm.nih.gov/pmc/articles/PMC3045642/.

sons—all the data is absolutely clear: Red-meat reducers eat much, much more chicken. For example, in the largest recent study, those who consumed the lowest amount of red meat ate 50 percent more chicken than those who consumed the most red meat.[5] Fifty percent more! The facts are clear: Anything at all that might possibly lead anyone to cut back on red meat actively harms animals.

Of course, we all know people who have gone veg for health reasons. As vegetarian advocates, we are obviously in a position to hear from and remember them. When we survey vegetarians (and/or meat reducers), of course we sometimes hear the "health argument" as a motivation. But looking only at vegetarians doesn't begin to show the full impact of any argument. The error is thinking the "health" vegetarians we know or survey are a true sample of society. They aren't. Rather, they represent a highly self-selected subsample.

History shows that eating fewer large animals and more small animals for health reasons isn't a made-up, worst-case scenario. It has been the driving force for the suffering and slaughter of billions and billions of birds. Just look at any graph of animals killed in the United States: As the consumption of mammals declined, the slaughter of chickens skyrocketed over the decades!

This is one of the reasons Vegan Outreach doesn't use

---

5 L. M. Aston, et al. "Meat Intake in Britain in Relation to Other Dietary Components and to Demographic and Risk Factor Variables: Analyses Based on the National Diet and Nutrition Survey of 2000/2001." *Journal of Human Nutrition and Dietetics* 26 (1), October 18, 2012.

any argument that could, in any way, support the general move toward giving up only red meat. Every person who decides to "eat better" more than counters the good done by a new vegetarian.

In other words, Vegan Outreach doesn't repeat anti-meat arguments. We promote pro-animal arguments. Obviously, it feels good to say that "vegans have lower rates of disease X." But the point isn't to feel good about ourselves or our diet. We're not out to justify or glorify our choices. Our goal is to keep as many animals from suffering as possible.

Of course, advocates can claim eating birds is bad for everyone's health and the environment. Putting aside the veracity of those health and environmental claims, this simply isn't the way the world works. People don't simply accept what a vegan advocate says as gospel truth. Rather, they combine what they hear from all sources, paying more attention to what their doctor and friends say. On top of this, people generally give much more weight to advice that leads toward what they want to do—i.e., continuing to eat the familiar and convenient foods their friends and family eat.

More importantly, we simply don't make decisions based on what is "perfect" for our health or the environment. None of us, vegans included, exercise the optimal amount, sleep the optimal amount, floss every day, work standing up, give up our car, etc. With few exceptions, we all follow our habits/peers. For most people (not a self-selected vegetarian subsample), if we change anything, we do something somewhat "better"—eating chickens instead of cows.

In other words, no matter what vegans claim is true or what we want, people will react from where they are, based on what they're used to and with an eye for what they want. No matter how strong we think our arguments are, no matter how noble our intentions or passionate our desires, when we advocate without considering human nature, history, and the numbers, we cause more animals to suffer and die.

If we want to help animals, we need to advocate for the animals.

Bad News for Red Meat Is Bad News for Chickens

Ginny Messina, RD

This piece originally appeared on The Vegan R.D. August 2011.[1]

Red meat has a bad PR problem. Two recent meta-analyses—one published in 2009 and one in 2011—linked red meat consumption to increased risk of colon cancer. In May [2011], the American Institute for Cancer Research and the World Cancer Research Fund reaffirmed conclusions from an earlier comprehensive report, saying that the evidence for a relationship between red meat and colon cancer is "convincing."

And it's not just cancer; a study published just last week found that adults who consume four ounces of red meat per day have a 20 percent increased risk for developing diabetes.

The evidence strongly suggests that it's a good idea

---

1 Ginny Messina, "Bad News for Red Meat is Bad News for Chickens," August 16, 2011: www.theveganrd.com/2011/08/bad-news-for-red-meat-is-bad-news-for-chickens.html.

for everyone to reduce their intake of red and processed meats. But from the animals' perspective, this is not necessarily great news. That's because many of these studies find that other animal foods—which can easily replace red meat in the diet—don't carry the same risks. There is no compelling body of evidence to suggest that eating white meat raises cancer risk, and some research suggests that replacing red meat with white meat lowers risk. (This is not to say that white meat is itself protective or has any particular health benefits. It's probably neutral and therefore lowers risk when it replaces harmful red meat.)

People are likely to react to news about the dangers of red and processed meats by replacing these foods with other meats—from fish and chickens—and in the process cause suffering to many, many more animals.

Assuming that one steer provides around 450 pounds of meat, a person eating a pound of beef per week would be responsible for the death of one steer every eight-and-a-half years or so. Replace that pound of beef a week with a pound of chicken (assuming that the average chicken yields two pounds of meat) and the number of animals killed would be about 220 chickens over the same time period. In fact, even if the health-conscious, meat-shunning consumer chose to reduce her meat intake by 75 percent—eating just four ounces of meat per week and getting all of it as chicken flesh—she would still be responsible for the death of more than fifty birds over that eight-and-a-half-year period.

And not only do more animals die when people replace red meat with chicken in their diet, but chickens and other birds live and die under conditions that are horrible even by the usual horrible standards of modern farming.

Red and processed meat consumption is a serious public health concern, and people need to know about the importance of reducing these foods in their diets. But publicizing every new study about the hazards of red meat doesn't promote veganism; it promotes animal suffering. A message about a vegan ethic, on the other hand, is a double win. It helps reduce animal suffering while also encouraging people to eliminate hazardous foods from their diets.

Edited on March 13, 2012: A study published online in the Archives of Internal Medicine[2] *found that all types of red meat are associated with increased risk for cancer and heart disease. Just three ounces a day of red meat was associated with a 13 percent increased risk of dying during the course of the study. The researchers also found that replacing red meat with poultry or low-fat dairy foods decreased risk as much or more than replacing it with legumes. This is another example of how a focus on the health risks of red meat in particular doesn't necessarily translate to a positive vegan message.*

---

2 A. Pan, et al. "Red Meat Consumption and Mortality; Results from 2 Prospective Cohort Studies." *Archives of Internal Medicine* (192) 7:555–63, April 9, 2012.

Postscript, December 2013; Ginny sends this quote: "A new study from Harvard School of Public Health (HSPH) researchers has found that red meat consumption is associated with an increased risk of total, cardiovascular, and cancer mortality. The results also showed that substituting other healthy protein sources, such as fish, poultry, nuts, and legumes was associated with a lower risk of mortality."[3]

---

3 "Red Meat Consumption Linked to Increased Risk of Total, Cardiovascular, and Cancer Mortality." Harvard School of Public Health News, March 12, 2012: http://bit.ly/1hqBY8z.

Why Vegan for Life Matters

2011

This article refers to the book Vegan for Life: Everything You Need to Know to Be Healthy and Fit on a Plant-Based Diet *by Jack Norris and Virginia Messina.*[1]

I have many regrets. One of the biggest is that my early days as a vegan were concerned mostly with saying how great veganism is and winning an argument with a meat eater, rather than actually helping animals. I am grateful to everyone who helped me get out of the vegan bubble.

I obviously understand wanting to believe the best about veganism, and I wanted to believe the siren song of appealing to self-interest to promote veganism. However, the idea that the majority of people will give up their familiar, favorite foods in order to benefit their long-term health has long shown itself to be unrealistic, at best. A simple survey of American's eating habits proves this beyond a shadow of a doubt.

---

1 References can be found at www.veganoutreach.org/advocacy/jacksbookmb.html.

Of course, the health argument isn't just a delusional attempt to trick the masses into going vegan. As pointed out before, it takes hundreds of intensively confined broiler chickens to provide the same number of meals as one steer. So even though the health argument has convinced some people to stop eating all animals, the others who move from beef and pork to chicken and fishes easily counter these new vegetarians. This, sadly, has led to many, many more animals being slaughtered, and has created much, much more suffering.

Still, many advocates have this seemingly unshakable, unfalsifiable belief that a vegan diet is so miraculous in its health benefits that there simply must be a way to convince the majority to go vegan. But the fantasy that veganism—and veganism alone—is the perfect diet isn't simply false, it is the exact opposite of many people's real-world experience.

When Jack Norris started leafleting around the country in 1995 and '96, he was surprised and frustrated by the number of former vegetarians and vegans who told him they had gone back to eating meat because they hadn't felt healthy as a vegetarian or vegan. This, of course, is completely counter to the standard vegan line that meat, eggs, and dairy are deadly poison, and being vegan will cure/prevent all manner of diseases.

How could this be? How could so many people feel so unhealthy as to go back to an animal-centered diet (feeling healthier upon doing so), when at the time, we knew, just knew, absolutely *knew* that being vegan was the only way to be healthy?

The tidal wave of failed vegetarians was so over-whelming that Jack, instead of rationalizing it away and staying in the vegan bubble, went back to school to become a registered dietitian. This way, he could read the actual original nutrition research, rather than merely seeing the selective vegetarian spin/distortion.

Jack's experience is backed up in this *Psychology Today* article, which indicates that 75 percent of people who go vegetarian in the United States eventually go back to eating animals.[2]

Seventy-five percent!

In other words, if everyone who went vegetarian had stayed vegetarian, there would be four times more vegetarians in the United States today! (A similar survey in the United Kingdom also showed more former vegetarians than current vegetarians there as well.)

And what did this poll find is the leading cause of people going back to eating animals? The existence of "happy meat"? No. Peer pressure? Nope. Missing the taste? Not even close.

The leading reason the vast majority of vegetarians go back to eating animals is because they didn't feel healthy.

Again, compare the real-world reality with the propaganda put out by many vegan advocates. An amazing disconnect!

It is, of course, easy for us to attack the people who

---

2 Hal Herzog, PhD, "Why Do Most Vegetarians Go Back to Eating Meat?" *Psychology Today*, June 20, 2011: www.psychologytoday.com/blog/animals-and-us/201106/why-do-most-vegetarians-go-back-eating-meat.

go back to eating meat. "They weren't really vegetarian!" "They weren't vegan!" "They weren't organic, non-GMO, whole-food vegans!" "They weren't raw!"

This can be initially satisfying ("Those quitters aren't as smart/dedicated as me! They just didn't go far enough!"). But here is the important question: Is our goal to feel good about our particular diet? Or do we want to help animals?

The only way to help animals is to help new people stop eating them. Attacking non-vegetarians—especially those who had been willing to alter their diet—is the exact opposite of helping animals! I deeply regret how long it took me to realize this.

To help new people take action to help animals, we must first accept their experience, rather than vilify them to rationalize our vegan mythology.

Understandably, many people are still keen to defend the vegan faith: "But I know the health argument works—just look at [near-vegan] Bill Clinton!"

In the first case, Bill Clinton proves the point (see Addendum 2). Secondly, a relative handful of self-selected individual examples can't counter the overall numbers: For every person out there saying he is vegetarian, there are three more saying, "Well, I used to be vegetarian, but . . ."

Any way you look at it, this is a disaster for the animals. They don't need us to glorify veganism. They need us to help new people make and sustain positive change. To do this, we need to face facts.

The facts are clear. The biggest net impacts health concerns have on the public's diet are the following:

1. Eating many, many more smaller animals.
2. Causing people to go back to their previous animal-centered diet.

The numbers are stark and unequivocal: When we promote the vegan health fantasy, overall we hurt animals.

Again, I have total sympathy with the desire to believe anything and everything claimed for veganism: It will cure cancer, reverse baldness, halt global warming, undo impotence, create world peace, and make us all much, much better looking.

But then I watch the latest video of the brutal, sickening barbarity inflicted on farmed animals.[3] And I know that no matter how much I want to buy into the feel-good fantasy about my personal veganism, it is infinitely more important to deal with the real world. Knowing the reality of what the animals are going through, as well as the reality of how most non-vegetarians actually react to different arguments, I am compelled to work for the biggest possible net impact for the animals, given the world as it really is and accepting the facts as they exist.

The way to have the biggest impact for the animals is simple:

1. Focus on the animals as the irrefutable bottom line: Buying meat, eggs, and dairy causes

---

3 See www.veganoutreach.org/video.

unnecessary suffering; we can each choose not to cause this suffering.

2. Provide people with honest, thorough, evidence-based information so they can change their diet and maintain that change.

The latter is why Jack and Ginny's *Vegan for Life*—and their work in general—is of vital importance.

We're not suggesting that big of a change. We simply need to stop saying that adopting an ethical diet is inherently healthier. Instead, while promoting ethical eating, we should let people know how healthful it can be to eat veg, and how to follow this healthy path. As Jack has said elsewhere:

> Every person who goes vegan and assumes it doesn't take any planning is at significant risk to have future poor health, leading them to end up quitting and telling others how their health failed as a vegan. My activism is basically dedicated to trying to stop this flow of ex-vegans who claim to have had poor health.
>
> Before I came along, any ex-vegan's story was simply countered by blaming them. What good does that do, other than to protect people's pre-conceived ideas? Here is a response to the ex-vegan phenomena that, in my opinion, can help people advocating for veganism. I hope that my work and my talks empower vegan advocates to be able to answer a lot of the nutrition questions they get, and with answers that are true and believable.

It is an absolute moral imperative that we learn and present the reality of vegan nutrition, so we can help new people stop eating animals, and stick with it.

The animals deserve no less.

ADDENDUM 1: EXTRAPOLATION

A personal note: I don't understand people who think there is one specific, detailed diet (types of foods, percentage of fat/protein/carbohydrate) that is absolutely and clearly optimal for every single person everywhere. How can we ignore the evidence of different people thriving on vastly different diets?

But beyond the evidence, just consider the reasoning. I have a chronic disease. If there were a very specific diet that controlled my symptoms, it would be optimal for me. But I would never think to claim that everyone simply must follow the diet that works for me!

For sixty-five years, Bill Clinton ate just about the worst diet possible. He did a great deal of damage to his body. Now he's much healthier eating a mostly plant-based diet. This is working for him, in his circumstances.

Even if loads of people were willing to adopt his very-low-fat, no-bread, no-nuts diet (which they never will), why would anyone think this was the optimal diet for, say, a four-year-old? Or a thirteen-year-old? Or a pregnant woman? Or a football player or ultramarathoner? And there is nothing to say that a different diet (and/or other lifestyle changes) wouldn't have also worked for Clinton. There is no control group in this situation.

Falling into the trap of unwarranted extrapolation isn't really an issue for Vegan Outreach members, who focus on the animals rather than trying to glorify their personal diet or denigrate everyone who doesn't eat/think just like them. But we should keep this in mind when we come across claims that apply to a specific population or circumstance.

ADDENDUM 2: A TARGET AUDIENCE OF ONE

I was recently asked if Bill Clinton's near-vegan diet proves that the "health argument" works.

Consider President Clinton's situation. He is very rich and powerful and can afford to have any chef prepare him anything he wants. He is very close to his outspoken daughter, who was an outspoken vegetarian for many years. Yet it still took extremely serious health problems (emergency surgery for a collapsed vein after quadruple bypass), his daughter's wedding, a desire to live to see grandchildren, and a personal friendship with several vegan doctors to get him to finally eat a more plant-based diet. (2013 update—the latest media coverage makes it clear President Clinton eats eggs and/or fish once a week. In other words, Clinton's case would indicate you can't really be vegan; you need to eat animals and animal products. Also, eating eggs and fish weekly causes more animals to die than someone who eats beef and dairy at every meal.)

So yes, it is clear that the health argument has some impact on rich, powerful men with vegan daughters, personal chefs, vegan doctors, and nearly fatal heart problems.

Of course, it's great to hear pseudo-veganism discussed positively (especially given the absurd attacks floating around), but we should not read more into this than is really there. Land animals are in deep trouble if significant changes in diets are limited to rich guys with personal chefs, vegan daughters and doctors, and severe health problems.

Lies, Damn Lies, and Statistics

2013

Let's be honest: People will lie to you.

They will lie to you to get your money. They'll lie to you to try to convince you to believe or follow them. They'll lie to you to build themselves up. They'll lie to you to win an argument.

And we know we'll lie to ourselves. We want to justify and support our beliefs. We want to prove ourselves right and believe we're smart.

Perhaps the most insidious form currently in vogue is manipulated but impressive-looking mathematics. This has been long known, of course. Thus, the saying, "Lies, damn lies, and statistics."

A great way to inoculate yourself to these manipulations is the book *Naked Statistics: Stripping the Dread from the Data* by Charles Wheelan—an engaging, funny, well-written survey of probability and statistics.

In the chapter "The Importance of Data," for example, Professor Wheelan covers the many forms of bias that sneak into data: selection bias, publication bias, recall bias, survivorship bias, and healthy user bias. Here, he discusses the last type:

> People who take vitamins regularly are likely to be healthy—because they are the kind of people who take vitamins regularly! Whether the vitamins have any impact is a separate issue. Consider the following thought experiment. Suppose public health officials promulgate a theory that all new parents should put their children to bed only in purple pajamas, because that helps stimulate brain development. Twenty years later, longitudinal research confirms that having worn purple pajamas as a child does have an overwhelmingly large positive association with success in life. We find, for example, that 98 percent of entering Harvard freshmen wore purple pajamas as children (and many still do) compared with only 3 percent of inmates in the Massachusetts state prison system.
>
> Of course, the purple pajamas do not matter; but having the kind of parents who put their children in purple pajamas does matter. Even when we try to control for factors like parental education, we are still going to be left with unobservable differences between those parents who obsess about putting their children in purple pajamas and those who don't. As *New York Times* health writer Gary Taubes explains, "At its simplest, the problem is that people who faithfully engage in activities that are good for them—taking a drug as prescribed, for instance, or eating what they believe is a healthy diet—are fundamentally different from those who don't." This effect can potentially con-

found any study trying to evaluate the real effect of activities perceived to be healthful, such as exercising regularly or eating kale. We think we are comparing the health effects of two diets: kale versus no kale. In fact, if the treatment and control groups are not randomly assigned, we are comparing two diets that are being eaten by two entirely different kinds of people. We have a treatment group that is different from the control group in two respects, rather than just one (125–26).

Equitable Ethics vs. Easy Environmentalism

The Essence of Earth Day

2008

> It is easy for us to criticize the prejudices of our grandfathers, from which our fathers freed themselves.
> It is more difficult to distance ourselves from our own views, so that we can dispassionately search for prejudices among the beliefs and values we hold.
> —Peter Singer, *Practical Ethics*

Many people express concern for the environment, and believe Earth Day is a good opportunity to draw attention to various issues. Sadly, yet not surprisingly, Earth Day has become largely a meaningless event, with just about everyone from the strictest vegan to the largest multinational claiming to support "the Earth."

But of course, the planet is in no danger. There is no way we can destroy a hunk of rock that weighs 13,000,000,000,000,000,000,000,000 pounds. That's thirteen septillion pounds.

Let me emphasize this point again, as it has generated

about as much angry feedback as anything I've ever written. "How can you say the Earth is in no danger?? What about fisheries' collapse/atmosphere pollution/rainforest destruction/topsoil erosion???" But none of these are "the Earth." The oceans could empty and the atmosphere blow away, and the planet would still exist. Only the razor-thin biosphere matters, because it is where we and our fellow feeling beings reside.

And this indicates what really is the bottom line: the lives of sentient beings. This is not something most people want to face, though. To avoid considering all our fellow creatures—and the implications they would have for our personal lives—many simply claim any and every environmental problem is equally pressing and anything "green" is equally commendable.

When you look at what has become of "environmentalism" in the United States, the emphasis is either on feeling good about ourselves ("I recycled!" "I bought a hybrid!") or condemning the "other" ("British Petroleum is evil!" "The government must do something about global warming!"). The avoidance of an honest, meaningful analysis of the fundamental bottom line isn't surprising. It is much simpler to parrot slogans, follow painless norms such as recycling, vilify faceless corporations, and demand that the government take action. All of this makes it easy to continue the status quo and still feel smugly green and good.

Our personal "environmentalism" is often nothing more than an expression of self-interest, just another laundry list of "we want." We want to feel good about ourselves for doing relatively painless things. We want charismatic megafauna to entertain us. We want wild spaces to use. We want clean air and water for our children.

But ethics aren't a question of what "we want." We can be truly thoughtful individuals and go beyond personal preferences, feel-good campaigns, and vilification of faceless others. We can each recognize that sayings and slogans are superficial, intentions and ideology irrelevant.

What matters isn't this rock we call Earth. What matters are the sentient beings who call this rock home. We can't care about "the environment" as though it is somehow an ethically relevant entity in and of itself. Rather, what matters are the impacts our choices have for our fellow feeling beings.

In the end, all that matters are the consequences our actions have for all animals.

All creatures—not just wild or endangered animals—desire to live free from suffering and exploitation. Cruelty is wrong, whether the victim is an eagle or a chicken, a wolf or a pig. The rest is just noise and obfuscation.

We simply can't consider ourselves ethical if we make choices that lead to more suffering for these creatures. And the greatest amount of suffering on Earth is caused when we choose to eat animals instead of a cruelty-free alternative.

Veganism is a statement against "we want." Veganism is the embodiment of a consistent, universal ethic. Veganism is a real choice with real consequences—a way to oppose and actively reduce violence, to make the world a truly better place for all. When we choose to live consistently and ethically as a vegan, we can look in the mirror knowing we are good people making choices that won't lead to more suffering for our fellow feeling beings.

But we know that being vegan is only the beginning. Those of us who are already vegan have many further opportunities to make the world a better place. Even if our food choices aren't directly causing animals to be slaughtered, our other choices—optimizing our example, time, and resources to have the greatest impact—have consequences even more important than what we eat.

This is why we are so honored to work with everyone who is a part of Vegan Outreach, where, in the best possible sense, every day is Earth Day.

Animals As the Bottom Line

Global Warming, Human Psychology, and Net Impact for Animals

Vegan Outreach Web site, 2008

At first blush, global warming seems to be a great hook for those of us promoting animal-friendly eating. But there are two problems:

1. OFFERING ACCURATE INFORMATION

Many vegans suggest meat is the leading cause of global warming. But this is not true. The production of meat is not the leading cause of greenhouse gases—only more than transportation. The following comes from a paper in *The Lancet* entitled "Food, Livestock Production, Energy, Climate Change, and Health":

> Although the main human source of greenhouse-gas emissions is combustion of fossil fuels for energy generation, non-energy emissions (including from agriculture and land-use changes) contribute more than

a third of the total greenhouse-gas emissions world-wide.[1]

Furthermore:

> Greenhouse-gas emissions from the agriculture sector account for about 22 percent of global total emissions; this contribution is similar to that of industry and greater than that of transport. Livestock production (including transport of livestock and feed) accounts for nearly 80 percent of the sector's emissions.

So livestock comes after energy generation and industry. And that is only globally. This next piece comes from *Salon*:

> Here in the US, livestock's impact is not quite so extreme: Six percent of our greenhouse gases come from livestock production, compared with 19 percent from cars, light trucks and airplanes.[2]

Very few meat eaters are actively seeking to eat vegetarian; rather, most people are looking for a reason to

---

1 McMichael, Anthony J. et al. Food, Livestock Production, Energy, Climate Change, and Health. *The Lancet* 370(9594): 1253–63, October 6, 2007. See <http://www.thelancet.com/journals/lancet/article/PIIS0140673607612562/abstract>

2 Liz Galst, "Earth to PETA," Salon.com, October 22, 2007: www.salon.com/2007/10/22/peta_2/. The entire article is definitely worth reading for how "informed" opinion plays out this issue.

dismiss us. When we exaggerate or lie, that is all that is remembered—not our other points or even the underlying reality. That worldwide meat production contributes more to global warming than all of transportation is accurate and striking; there is no reason to exaggerate.

2. THE EXPECTED IMPACT IN THE PUBLIC MIND AND HOW IT ACTUALLY AFFECTS ANIMALS

When the public hears "livestock" (as in "livestock causes more global warming than transportation"), they think cattle, and the conclusion is that they should eat less beef. Even when people hear "meat . . . global warming," they think of burping (or flatulent) cows. (Of course, the news is written by, and the media run by, meat eaters. They will always choose the side that is least challenging to their habits/the status quo.)

For those who look into the science and aren't already vegan, concern for global warming leads almost inevitably to more chickens being eaten (it takes approximately 200 chickens to provide the same number of meals as one steer).

For example, the *Salon* article referenced above reports:

> "Astonishingly enough," says study coauthor Gidon Eshel, a Bard College geophysicist, "the poultry diet is actually better than lacto-ovo vegetarian." In other words, a roast chicken dinner is better for the planet than a cheese pizza.

How about going vegan?

The average American is responsible for about 26 tons annually, so if the entire US population went vegan, we'd reduce our greenhouse gas emissions by only 6 percent.

The vast majority of that 6 percent is from cutting out beef and dairy.

Similarly, an article in *Environmental Science and Technology* entitled "Food-Miles and the Relative Climate Impacts of Food Choices in the United States" notes the following:

Different food groups exhibit a large range in GHG [greenhouse gas] intensity; on average, red meat is around 150 percent more GHG-intensive than chicken or fish. Thus, we suggest that dietary shift can be a more effective means of lowering an average household's food-related climate footprint than "buying local." Shifting less than one day per week's worth of calories from red meat and dairy products to chicken, fish, eggs, or a vegetable-based diet achieves more GHG reduction than buying all locally sourced food.[3]

---

3 Christopher L. Weber and H. Scott Matthews, "Food-Miles and the Relative Climate Impacts of Food Choices in the United States," *Environmental Science Technology* 42(10): 3508–13, 2008: http://psufoodscience.typepad.com/psu_food_science/files/es702969f.pdf.

The *Los Angeles Times* shows "replace beef with chicken" in action:

> "No hamburger patties?" asked an incredulous football player, repeating the words of the grill cook. He glowered at the posted sign: 'Cows or cars? Worldwide, livestock emits 18 percent of greenhouse gases, more than the transportation sector! Today we're offering great-tasting vegetarian choices.' "Just give me three chicken breasts, please," he said.[4]

Global warming and diet is an argument that makes sense to us vegans and makes us think, "Here is a great, self-interested hook I can use to convince others of veganism's superiority!" But it isn't a question of whether veganism is the best diet for addressing global warming. The bottom line has to be the actual impact of the message we choose to present. In other words, we shouldn't seek out and use arguments that seem to support veganism—veganism isn't the point. If we take suffering seriously, we must seek to present a message that reduces the most suffering.

As Nobel Prize–winning economist Herbert Simon discovered, human psychology and decision making are generally determined by "good enough." People don't hear about a concern (especially a relatively abstract issue like global warming) and take it to the fullest extent—

---

4 Kenneth R. Weiss, "With Low-Carbon Diets, Consumers Step to the Plate," *Los Angeles Times*, April 22, 2008: http://articles.latimes.com/2008/apr/22/local/me-lowcarbon22.

e.g., stop driving entirely—but rather, those motivated enough will do something (drive a bit less, drive a more fuel-efficient car) and feel good that they are doing something.

In this case, though, doing "something" means eating a lot more chickens. We can say, "But being vegan is even better!" until we're blue in the face, but experience shows that this is effective only in the rarest of cases. The vast majority of people who will be moved at all about global warming are happy to be "taking action" by eating a lot more chickens. And it is the cattle industry that is worried about the global-warming-diet argument, not the poultry industry. The latter loves anything and everything that badmouths beef.

Although the global warming–food connection seems clear to us, what actually matters is how the argument plays out in non-vegans' minds. When used on its own, the diet/global-warming angle can easily do more harm (increase in chickens eaten) than good (people going veg).

Instead of an oblique anti-beef message, we can present a direct anti-cruelty/pro-animal message, and convince more people to move toward eating fewer or no animals. For this reason, I think we should be very careful how we use global warming. It is a hot topic, so it gives us an "in" with the media and environmental groups. But presented on its own, the case will very often have the bottom line of more chickens dying, given human psychology. The global warming–diet connection can work as a hook to capture attention and allow us to draw attention to the horrors of modern agribusiness, with a special focus on cruelty to chickens.

Postscript

On a related topic, there is growing recognition that increased usage of certain biofuels will exacerbate global hunger.[5] Of course, the same argument of resource usage can be made regarding using crops as animal feed.[6] According to the Food and Agriculture Organization (FAO), only 100 million metric tons (tonnes) of cereal crops go to biofuel, while 760 million metric tons go to animal feed—and the latter figure isn't even counting soy:

> There is plenty of food. It is just not reaching human stomachs. Of the 2.13bn tonnes likely to be consumed this year, only 1.01bn, according to the United Nations' Food and Agriculture Organization, will feed people. . . . But there is a bigger reason for global hunger, which is attracting less attention only because it has been there for longer. While 100m tonnes of food will be diverted this year to feed cars, 760m tonnes will be snatched from the mouths of humans to feed animals—which could cover the global food deficit 14 times. If you care about hunger, eat less meat.[7]

---

5 See, for instance, C. Ford Runge and Benjamin Senauer's "How Biofuels Could Starve the Poor," *Foreign Affairs*, May/June, 2007: http://fam.ag/JAVZOE.

6 See "Resources and Contamination" at http://bit.ly/JAW4St.

7 See George Monbiot, "The Pleasures of the Flesh," Monbiot.com, April 15, 2008: http://bit.ly/JAW8Sh. For more on Monbiot's "evolution," see Dr. Matthew Cole's "Murder: A Benign Extravagance?" *The Vegetarian* (Winter 2010): http://bit.ly/1mByuXx.

Keep in mind, however, that beef is much, much less efficient than chicken (and eggs)—see, again, the *Salon* article:

> Welcome, then, the savior of environmentally concerned carnivores everywhere: the chicken. Unlike cattle, chickens don't burp methane. They also have an amazing ability to turn a relatively small amount of grain into a large amount of protein. A chicken requires 2 pounds of grain to produce a pound of meat, compared with about 6 pounds of grain for a feedlot cow and 3 pounds for a pig. Poultry waste produces only about one-tenth of the methane of hog and cattle manure.

Like thousands of activists over the past decades, I'd love to think there is some perfect, logical, self-interested argument that won't just vindicate my veganism but also actually convince large numbers of people to go vegan, while not leading others to eat more chickens. But this is not the case—there just aren't lots of people out there who secretly want to be vegan but just need that one statistic. For nearly everyone, any change away from the status quo is difficult and resisted. As much as we'd love to argue otherwise, in response to health or environmental arguments, the first, easiest, and most convenient and socially acceptable step is to eat more chickens.

It is worth briefly considering why health and environmental arguments seem to be more easily "accepted" by people, and why most individuals are resistant and defensive when faced with the cruelty argument. Much of this could well be that health choices are personal (and easily overridden by habit and convenience, even in the face of severe health issues), while environmental concerns are abstract and easily assuaged by taking some minor action (new lightbulbs, recycling).

The obvious cruelty and vicious brutality of factory farms, however, is both real, immediate, undeniable, and clearly an ethical challenge to our view of ourselves. For these reasons, the animals' suffering can't be easily dismissed and forgotten. Thus, it is important for meat eaters to avoid the issue as much as possible (and to make the messenger the issue, whenever possible). For the same reason, it is incumbent on us, as animal advocates, to actually advocate the animals' case, so that no one can avoid facing the hidden reality.

In deciding what to present to the public, our criterion shouldn't be, "Does this seem (to me) to denigrate (some) meat and/or support veganism?" We shouldn't be trying to justify our diet—we need to stand up for the animals. We don't get to determine how people should react; we must consider how our chosen argument will actually play out among the general public and through the media. We must set aside our personal biases and needs and honestly ask, "Is this the argument that will alleviate as much suffering as possible?" The animals are counting on us.

Specialize and Network

Anne Green

*Vegan Outreach Director of
Development and Programs
2008*

Vegan Outreach is dedicated to reducing suffering as much as possible.

To this end, we strive to be as efficient as possible. In the early days, being efficient meant that Matt, Jack, and I hand-collated, stapled, and folded thousands of booklets. Thankfully, our outreach has outgrown our living room! But our emphasis on efficiency continues.

A large part of being efficient is specialization. Vegan Outreach specializes in distributing compelling booklets to young people at colleges and universities across North America, with a determined focus on reaching undergraduates in the United States.

The "Programs" part of my work involves making sure activists have the resources they need to accomplish this mission. This includes providing the booklets themselves, of course, but also ensuring access to information, housing, and help. To do this efficiently, I coordinate with activists, network with organizations, collect and record data, and bring all the information together.

We coordinate with national and regional groups—e.g., The Humane League, Mercy for Animals, Compassionate Action for Animals, Animal Protection and Rescue League, and others—as well as with local and student groups (Vegas Veg, Bay Area Veg, UCONN Veg, and many, many others) so that the maximum number of people can be reached with minimal duplication of effort.

Also, I contact our helpful hosts for traveling activists. Our Hotel Vegan Outreach network is made up of the finest "innkeepers" on the continent! (Many of them also take in massive shipments of booklets.) And they open their homes not only for our Adopt a College leafleters, but also for the traveling Warped Tour team. (Imagine having a crew of tired and hungry activists, who leafleted all day in the summer sun, knock on your door late at night!)

I follow up with people who order Vegan Outreach booklets, not only to make sure they've received their order, but also to put them in touch with other activists in their area whenever possible. The more connections we make, the more people we can reach, and the more people will stop eating animals!

Furthermore, I keep track of the data from activists' reports: Who distributes booklets where, and when? Who grants permission at a private school? Where is the best place to park, to stand—and even to eat—at colleges and universities across North America?

Of course, Vegan Outreach shares this information

via our Adopt a College site, so activists across North America can access it quickly and easily. This helps all activists conduct efficient outreach, even in a new place.

Vegan Outreach provides the hub—the outreach material and the data necessary to know who, what, where, when, and how. Our networks of groups, organizations, individuals, hosts, and helpers across the continent are the spokes.

Vegan Outreach specializes and networks so no one has to reinvent the wheel. Rather, we can be the wheel. And we can drive the movement forward efficiently, creating positive progress for the animals.

V.
THE
FUTURE

One Possible Future

A Roadmap to Animal Liberation

Vegan Outreach eNewsletter, March 2007

With cruelty rampant on factory farms, and vegetarians currently a small minority, it is easy to dismiss the hope for a vegetarian world as naïve. "My Uncle Dick hunts, and my cousin Jeb is always mocking me for being vegan. You're crazy if you think they will ever change!"

These are legitimate concerns. However, it is nevertheless possible to achieve our goals—and much more quickly than we imagine.

Taking a longer perspective can help guide our advocacy. Society has advanced an incredible amount in just the last few centuries. Even though democracy was first proposed in ancient Greece, only during the eighteenth century did humanity see the hints of a democratic system. Only recently was slavery abolished in the industrialized world. Not until the last hundred years was child labor ended in Europe and North America, child abuse criminalized, women allowed to vote. Some minorities have attained more equal rights only in the last few decades.

It is hard to comprehend just how much society has changed in recent history. Prejudices we can hardly fathom today were completely accepted just decades ago. For example, if we read what was written and said about slavery—fewer than 150 years ago—the defenders were not just ignorant racists, but admired politicians, civic and religious leaders, and learned intellectuals. What is horrifying to us now was once not only accepted, but respected.

However slow our progress may feel, we are advancing at lightning speed compared to past social justice movements. A century ago, almost no animals received any protection whatsoever from abuse. Now, according to a 2003[1] Gallup poll, 96 percent of Americans want to see animals protected from abuse, 62 percent want strict laws regulating the treatment of farmed animals, and fully one-fourth believe that animals deserve "the exact same rights as people to be free from harm and exploitation." Until 1990, there was one ballot initiative to protect animals that had passed at a state level—just one! Since 1990, animal advocates have passed more than twenty, including several directly abolishing some of the worst abuses on factory farms.

Today the vast majority of people oppose cruelty to animals, and many question eating animals, at least on some level.[2] Thus, the discussion now must focus on

---

1 David W. Moore, "Public Lukewarm on Animal Rights," Gallup, May 21, 2003: www.gallup.com/poll/8461/public-lukewarm-animal-rights.aspx.

2 In 2011, Grist's Tom Laskawy reviewed a survey from agribusiness front group Center for Food Integrity: "The study's analysis notes

helping people see that eating meat violates their own principles. This effort is only just beginning. Twenty years ago, most animal advocacy in the United States was focused on fur and vivisection, nearly ignoring the roughly 99 percent of animals butchered for food. Only recently have more groups and individuals focused on this 99 percent by exposing the cruelty of factory farms and promoting vegetarianism. The first systematic national effort to reach the best audience—Vegan Outreach's Adopt a College program—was launched fewer than four years ago!

In large part because of this shift in advocacy, factory farms—which most people knew nothing about ten or twenty years ago—are now considered ethical abominations to many. Bruce Friedrich and I acknowledge this in *The Animal Activist's Handbook*:

> Twenty years ago, few people had heard the word "vegan." Finding mock meats and soymilk was nearly impossible. According to market research by Mintel, "Until the mid-1990s, change was slow in coming to the world of vegetarian foods, and many average consumers relegated 'vegetarian products' to a counter-cultural movement, not a mainstream trend" (85).

---

that 51 percent strongly agree that they have 'no problem' eating meat and dairy. It's still a majority, but the number is down a full 12 percent since 2007. The trend suggests that by 2012, less than a majority of consumers will strongly agree that eating animals or animal products is okay. Are Americans getting ready to let their vegan flag fly?" "Consumers Losing Faith in Big Food," November 4, 2011: http://bit.ly/1mBzP0s.

Today, even cousin Jeb doesn't need "vegan" explained to him. You can find veggie burgers, soy milk, and various other vegetarian convenience foods in most grocery stores. As Bruce and I add, "According to Mintel, 'In 2003, the vegetarian foods market in the US topped $1.6 billion in sales. This represents a constant-price growth rate of 111.3 percent since 1998.' Mintel estimates that the market was up to $2.8 billion in 2006."

Forbes reports the following:

Market research shows that the number of consumers who lean toward some sort of vegetarianism is increasing across all age groups. The Vegetarian Resource Group estimates that 2.8% of adult Americans consider themselves vegetarian, up from 2.3% in a 2000 survey. Another 6% to 10% of the population said it was "almost vegetarian" and another 20% to 25% are "vegetarian inclined," or intentionally reducing meat in their diet, according to VRG.[3]

According to Food Systems Insider, "Ten percent of 25- to 34-year-olds say they never eat meat."

---

3 Mark Tatge, "Vegetarian Sales Get Meaty," *Forbes*, September 15, 2004: www.forbes.com/2004/09/15/cz_mt_0915organic.html. 2014 update: "The meat-free market is growing, with about 7% of population now calling themselves vegetarian or vegan, according to a recent Gallup poll. And yet, 43% of the population eats vegetarian meals at least once a week." See Maggie Hennessey's "Honey, Let's Have Vegan Tonight," FoodNavigator-usa.com, January 15, 2014: www.foodnavigator-usa.com/Manufacturers/Honey-let-s-have-vegan-tonight.

As we continue our efforts, more vegetarian products arrive on the market every month. Having convenient vegetarian options available is vital, as it makes it easier for new people to try—and, more importantly, to stick with—a compassionate diet. As more people sample vegetarian meats and other vegetarian products, competition will continue to increase the supply and variety, improving quality and driving down prices. This cycle of growing numbers of vegetarians and the increasing convenience of vegetarian eating is self-reinforcing. Essentially, the technology of vegetarian meats and other foods is both driven by and a driver of moral progress.

If we continue to expand our advocacy, the growth of vegetarianism will accelerate to a tipping point, where opposition to factory farms and the adoption of vegetarianism become the "norms" among influential groups. Legislation, as it usually does, will continue to follow these evolving norms, and we'll see more of animal agriculture's worst practices outlawed and abolished—something that has already begun. Corporate practices will also continue to adjust to the demands of an increasingly aware market.

At the same time, powerful economic forces will kick in because meat is ultimately inefficient. It is more efficient to eat plant foods directly, rather than feeding plant foods to animals and then eating some of the animals' flesh. Of course, people aren't going to substitute tofu for meat, but that is not the choice they'll be making. Food science has advanced such that the best vegetarian meats are able to satisfy even hardcore carnivores. Deli slices from Tofurky, burgers from Boca, Gimme Lean sausage and ground beef, Morningstar MealStarters, Garden-burger's Riblets and Chik'n—all of these dismiss the notion that giving up meat is necessarily a deprivation.

The faster the growth in the number of people eating vegetarian, the faster vegetarian meats will improve in taste, become cheaper, and be found in far more places. (Compare a 2006 Boca Burger to a 1986 Nature Burger, and imagine how good a 2026 veggie burger will be!) In addition, *in vitro* meats become more viable each year. *In meatro* can also be more efficient than actual animal corpses, and can be engineered to have the same bene-fits as vegetarian meats: no cholesterol, good fats (ome-ga-3s), no factory farms, no slaughterhouses, no manure ponds, no greenhouse-gas emissions, no food poisoning, no mad cow, no avian flu. These technologies will also be accelerated by the growth of vegetarianism.

Our challenge now is to expand the vegetarian mar-ket by explaining to more meat eaters the reasons for choosing vegetarian meals, while exposing them to new—though similar—products. The more rapidly we do this, the sooner cruelty-free eating will be widespread.

After his first heart attack, Uncle Dick will shift over to vegetarian meats that have no cholesterol or saturated or trans fats and are high in omega-3s. Cousin Jeb's sec-ond wife—a vegetarian since being handed an *Even If You Like Meat* booklet at college in 2003—will use that as an excuse to only cook vegetarian meals, and Jeb will hardly notice the difference! Their daughter Barbara will grow up a vegan activist and will oversee McDonald's shift to non-animal chicken in their sandwiches.

Despite the current horror and continued suffering,

if we take the long view and are willing to commit to the work that needs to be done, we should be deeply optimistic. Animal liberation can be the future. With our efforts, it could be achieved with a whimper, not a bang. Change comes not by revolution, but through person-by-person outreach progressing hand in hand with advances in technology, leading slowly but inexorably to a new norm that, to most people, hardly seems different. But an unfathomable amount of suffering will be prevented.

It is up to us to make this happen.

2013 Follow-up:
I came across this restaurant review on Yelp:

> Wish they were in my neighborhood, 'cause I'd be one happy fat vegan cat eating some deep fried tofu with their crazy good tartar sauce, some slap yo' mama good greens and getouttahere delicious, amazing mac and cheese. (Hint: do not eat this garlicy goodness mac and cheese before a date.) But on the serious? I'm a carnivore all the way, and I swear to the Gods above if Souley Vegan was in my 'hood I'd be eating vegan more days a week than I'd ever eat meat. This food is the shizznyee. Not kidding.

The vegan future is here. It is just unevenly distributed. We will change that.

A New World, Piece by Piece

with Jack Norris

Originally appeared in Vegan Outreach's eNewsletter June 2007

Vegan Outreach exists to reduce, as much as possible, the amount of suffering in the world. Veganism, rights, and liberation are not goals in and of themselves—they are merely tools to reduce suffering.

Given our desire to reduce suffering, of course we want a vegan world. Yet while a compassionate, vegan society is the ideal, our mission to reduce suffering must be more than hoping for a perfect world at some point in the future. If we truly take suffering seriously, we must work for a better world now. Hundreds of billions of animals will be raised and slaughtered for food before we can ever possibly achieve widespread veganism. We must not ignore the suffering of those animals who will certainly exist and endure agony.

From decades of outreach to millions of people, we have found that very few individuals respond to abstract, intellectual (animals have natural rights) or absolutist (vegan-only) positions. People do respond, though, when shown the cruelty inherent in modern agribusiness, which is why Vegan Outreach focuses on these abuses.

It is reasonable to wonder whether focusing on cruelty supports the sale of less inhumane meat by implying that it is OK to eat non-factory-farmed animals. Our long experience has clearly shown that focusing on how animals are raised and killed is the best way to maximize both the number of people who oppose factory farms as well as those who eventually oppose killing animals altogether. Exposing the manifest yet hidden cruelty of modern agribusiness is the best way to get the most people to open their hearts and minds to the animals' plight.

As we work to expose the hidden realities of factory farms, some people will stop eating animals. But others will still be unwilling to go veg. There is no way around this. The meat, egg, and dairy industries recognize this, too, and play to consumers' feelings with labels like "humane" and "animal-care certified." Big ag will do this whether we like it or not; vegans don't own words like "humane." As much as we might wish otherwise, we can't keep agribusiness from using any word for its own purposes.

Because some meat eaters will inevitably react to our education efforts by seeking out animals raised in conditions less horrible than on standard factory farms, people in a position to do so should take any opportunity to make sure industry labels are meaningful. Then, discomforted consumers not yet willing to go veg will be able to take real steps to reduce suffering. Changing one's diet because of a concern for suffering very often represents only the first step in an ethical evolution.

Remember, very few current vegans went from a standard American diet to vegan overnight.

It is, of course, frustrating when people offer "humane"-labeled meat as their excuse not to go veg. We must remember, though, that most people have offered and will continue to offer some excuse to continue eating animals, regardless of what we do. We can't ignore the suffering of billions of farmed animals just to deny people one possible excuse among many. Our concern for reducing suffering must extend beyond promoting only veganism. If we take suffering seriously, we must support efforts to abolish cages, crates, forced molting through starvation, and electrical incapacitation at slaughter. We can't wish for more cruelty in the hope that our case for veganism is "stronger."

Instead of simply wishing for or "demanding" a different world, we must honestly evaluate the world as it currently is, and then do our very best to reduce as much suffering as possible. We must reach and influence the people who might currently be willing to go vegan; reach and influence people who might currently be willing to go vegetarian; reach and influence the people who won't (now) go veg, but who might stop buying meat from factory farms—and help support all of these people as they continue to evolve as consumers.

Outreach efforts to all of these people are necessary if we are to help a large and diverse society evolve to a new ethical norm. This is why Vegan Outreach produces a range of literature to make everyone and anyone, in any situation, the most effective advocate for animals possible. While we are each able to do this outreach in our local areas, we support—and certainly don't waste our limited time opposing—the efforts of large organizations to bring about the abolition of the worst abuses on factory farms. Each step brings the animals' interests to light, making people consider the otherwise hidden reality behind the meat they eat. There is no other way to go from a carnivorous society, where farmed animals have virtually no protection, to a vegan society where they have near-total protection.

For every cage emptied and every person convinced to change their diet, we realize there is more work to be done to reduce suffering. The industry also recognizes that all these efforts are progress toward our ultimate goal; agribusiness journal *Feedstuffs* (April 2, 2007) editorialized it this way:

> Very recent developments would suggest that producers are now losing. If producers are losing, others are also losing—everyone who has a stake in dairy, meat and poultry production. . . . [I]t's not about animal welfare. It's not about cages and stalls. . . . It's about raising animals for food, and the activists' agenda is to end the practice. It will take decades, but they are the ones who are winning—piece by piece by piece.

Radical Pragmatism

A VO Manifesto

2013

VO recently received an e-mail from someone who refuses to use our advocacy booklets because they don't demand pure veganism. This was our reply.

Thanks so much for your e-mail. You make a very, very important point: "I became vegan as a result of being an animal liberation activist. I'm not a vegan activist."

That is Vegan Outreach's position, too. We don't seek to promote a particular diet. We are not slaves to a certain philosophy or dogma. We are only seeking to lessen the animals' suffering—period. And in this—recognizing the diversity of people and the frailties of human psychology in order to do our absolute best for the animals—we are radical, hardcore pragmatists.

It is easy to think the only way to help the animals is solely to promote a pure, animal-exploitation-free existence. The obvious and straightforward rationalization is, "I'm vegan for the animals; therefore, everyone should be vegan for the animals!"

And if everyone were as thoughtful, courageous, and dedicated as you, then of course VO's approach would be different—and our task much, much easier!

But you know and I know that you are an outlier. Just go to the your schools' food court. Go to a football game. Head over to Disneyland—there aren't loads of people exactly like you. There are lots of good, ethical people around, but they aren't currently willing to stand out from the crowd, to go against their friends and habits. They aren't able to change their lives entirely and all at once, based on our current personal philosophy. And yet those are the people we have to reach, if we are to create a truly better world for the animals.

It really is a problem for us vegans—perhaps our biggest. We are often more concerned that the message meets our current personal standards and sounds good to us, rather than being the optimal message for having new people start to take action to help the animals. But if we think about it for just a second, having a "pure" message is far from the best thing we can do for the animals.

I understand the urge, of course. I used to be driven by words and dogma. I used to think we couldn't give people an "out" or an "excuse" to eat animals by talking about anything other than absolute veganism. Really, though, my prior attitude is nearly laughable. People don't need an "out" to eat animals—they already eat animals.

Indeed, by presenting a seemingly unachievable "pure vegan" standard, we actually give people an "out" to ignore the animals' plight altogether. Insisting on a message that conveys our current conscience can hurt the animals—actively and significantly—relative to a more realistic, step-wise approach. The psychological research shows this, but far more importantly our experience of the past quarter century has shown the truth of this over and over again.

You would be shocked—truly amazed—at how many people are suddenly interested when we—Vegan Outreach activists—admit that not all products or farms are equally cruel. People who had been entirely dismissive will perk right up when we don't insist they have to be vegan right now—that everyone can help animals, even if they currently believe they can't be vegan. The vast majority of the many tens of thousands of people who have changed from recent Vegan Outreach booklets have been those who started to evolve—who took the first step—because of our pragmatic and psychologically sound approach, our total focus on the animals, not a particular diet or dogma.

We know it is far easier to get ten people to eat only half as many animals, compared to convincing two people to go fully and immediately vegan. More importantly, the animals are far, far better off in the former case, especially if we continue to provide realistic and pragmatic support so people can continue to evolve.

Again, this isn't conjecture. We constantly get feedback like what we just ran in the blog:

> I received *Even If You Like Meat . . . You Can Help End This Cruelty* from your organization (actually my daughter was given this book while on a college campus). I think so many people get discouraged because

they have a hard time sticking with a vegan lifestyle, so I thought this book was very relevant because even if someone still eats some meat at least they could cut back, and then maybe eventually they would make the switch to a vegan lifestyle.

We can either dismiss people like this as weak and unworthy of our consideration. Or we can recognize they are the key to our progress toward animal liberation!

None of what I've said here is Vegan Outreach's dogma—rules to which we've been wedded. These are all lessons we've learned over the years—after mistakes that, ultimately, failed the animals at the time. In the end, it took me quite a while to develop the courage to set aside my personal wants and demands, and instead pursue what is best for the animals, given the world as it is, and people as they are.

Indeed, we fail the animals when we refuse to learn from our—and others'—past mistakes, when we fail to recognize that not everyone will go vegan immediately and perfectly. We can only do our best for the animals when we try to work with everyone where they are, and do our best to get them to take the first step.

That is Vegan Outreach's dogma.

"Together, We Will Make the Next Twenty Years Even More Amazing!"

2013

Anyone who's read Jack's history of Vegan Outreach[1] knows that when he and I met, we adopted the "do something, do anything" approach. If something was in the news, we would protest it. If a high-profile case of abuse made us angry, we would write letters. Even when I met Anne Green, my main goal was to get more people to protests.

But the three of us eventually realized that since we obviously can't do everything, we had better make sure our limited time and money helps as many animals as possible, even if the animals aren't high profile.

It simply comes down to this: If we want a vegan world, we have to convince people to stop eating animals. There's no way around this. There are no shortcuts.

For twenty years, we have expanded and refined

---

1 Jack Norris, "A History of Vegan Outreach and Our Influences," Vegan Outreach, 2009: www.veganoutreach.org/articles/history.html.

our work, updated our information, and optimized our procedures. The three of us prompt each other to stay focused on our singular goal: to help as many people as possible take the first step to help animals, and then the next step, and then the next step.

But we don't simply want more vegetarians and vegans. We want more effective advocates out there, accelerating the spread of compassion.

I don't know how many of you were vegan in 1993, but let me tell you, 2013 is far, far better than ever I imagined it could be back then. Seriously—it is simply amazing. All the people who are vegan, the daily news coverage of factory farms, the plethora of vegetarian restaurants, products, and options—it is just incredible. And of course, the bottom line is the number of animals killed in the United States has been declining ever since Vegan Outreach first distributed a million booklets in a year in 2006. As I said: amazing.

Of course, I know we see heartbreaking news all the time. But because of so many people's commitment to Vegan Outreach, we are creating real, lasting change every day! I am truly honored to be a part of this amazing work with so many incredible individuals. Together, we will make the next twenty years even more amazing!

Better

December, 2013

2013 was a very good year for Vegan Outreach—so good that the meat industry continues to find it unbelievable that all of us, working together, reached nearly a million students during fall semester![1]

Thank you so much for being such a key part of this work.

As is always the case, we are working to make next year even better. To have the biggest impact possible per dollar donated and hour worked, Vegan Outreach strives for focused, efficient outreach. Obviously, we don't claim that leafleting is the only effective form of advocacy or the only thing worth doing—there are great groups doing important, amazing work out there, and we continue to support and work with them so everyone can be as effective as possible, so that society can continue to evolve on all possible fronts.

---

1 See "Bonus: Big Ag Can't Believe It!" December 13, 2013: http://bit.ly/millionstudents or "Vegan Outreach Continues to Drive the Meat Industry Crazy!" December 26, 2013: http://bit.ly/DanCrazy.

But the bottom line remains this simple fact: To create the truly fundamental change we want, we have to change society from the bottom-up, person by person. Vegan Outreach knows that for this to happen, every young person needs to learn the reality of modern agriculture—and the details of making informed, sustainable, compassionate choices—before they fall into the more fixed routines of adult life. We need to reach all the young people of today because they will determine society tomorrow. We can't count on all of them to click a link or come across a video or news report. We need to go directly to them and put the information right into their hands.

The meat industry knows this, which is why they are so threatened by our work together.

I'm amazed at the progress we've made in the past twenty years. And as I have written elsewhere, our efforts together will make the future even better. Better than we can currently imagine!

I am truly and deeply grateful to be a part of this work with you. I absolutely do not take it for granted. All the talk and plans mean nothing without you and your support. Your donations have printed the booklets, created new vegetarians, and rippled out, creating the fundamentally new world we both want.

So I thank you—I am far more grateful for and appreciative of your thoughtful, dedicated generosity than I can possibly begin to express.

Together, we'll make 2014 the best year yet!

A Meaningful Life

Introduction by John Oberg

Remembering when your life changed is often a blurred, fuzzy memory at best. True inspiration usually comes in a fleeting moment that is difficult to reflect back on. I'm fortunate, however, to remember the exact moment my life took a turn for the better—a turn for a more meaningful existence.

It was October 2009. My friend Rachael and I had gone from vegetarian to vegan after discovering the horrors of factory farming. We embraced the change and the challenge but knew there was more to be done for animals than by simply being vegan. I was vaguely familiar with activism but knew nothing of tactics, strategies, or effectiveness. I wanted to learn more.

I pulled up Google and began my quest for knowledge. My thirst was insatiable, and luckily for me the stars must have aligned, as I somehow fell upon the Vegan Outreach homepage. I wasn't familiar with the group but was drawn in immediately. To my delight, I discovered the list of advocacy essays and articles in its own section of their Web site. How perfect! What else could a new activist hope for than a little bit of guidance?

I began reading. And reading. And rereading. I thought to myself, "Wow, if I'm going to take activism seriously, I need to engage in X, not Y. There's only so much I can do in my finite time here—I want to make the best of it." With my jaw on the floor and butterflies in my stomach, I continued reading. Upon completion of this short essay entitled "A Meaningful Life," I came to the immediate realization that this was the blueprint for making the biggest impact, dollar for dollar, hour for hour. This pragmatic, selfless approach excited me. Before this, I thought I was going to have to break into factory farms and steal live animals to make a difference. These few thousand words made me realize that the best approach was perhaps the less obvious one: A patient, sensible approach was what was needed above all else.

If we truly care about animals' interests, every activist has a duty to consider paths to making the biggest impact with our limited time and resources. Objectively looking at the options and ideas, the key points that Matt Ball drives home in this stellar piece of writing are the exact points we need to prioritize and take seriously. Many of the best activists I know drew their inspiration and followed their path directly because of reading "A Meaningful Life." Now, they're living some of the most meaningful lives possible.

If the voiceless animals were given a voice, they'd ask and thank you for taking this pragmatic approach into consideration. We owe it to ourselves to examine our options and owe it to the animals to put their interests first.

Enjoy the following essay that means so much to me and so much to many others. The animals don't have much going for them, but this piece of writing is one of the few things that will be at their backs until the day this work is no longer necessary.

—John Oberg

A Meaningful Life

Making a Real Difference in Today's World

Everyone who wants to make the world a better place faces the same challenge: opening people's hearts and minds to new ideas.

THE BOTTOM LINE

Those who are successful in making the world a better place are students of human nature. They understand that each of us is born with a certain intrinsic nature, raised to follow specific beliefs, and taught to hold particular prejudices. Over time, we discover new "truths" and abandon others, altering our attitudes, principles, and values.

Even though we can recognize that our belief system changes over time, at any given point, most of us believe our current opinions are "right"—our convictions well founded, our actions justified. We each want to think we are, at heart, a good person. Even when, years later, we find ourselves reflecting on previously held beliefs with a sense of bemusement (or worse), it rarely occurs to us that we may someday feel the same way toward the attitudes we now hold.

Effective advocates understand this evolution of people's views, and, furthermore, recognize they can't change anyone's mind. No matter how elegant an argument, real and lasting change comes only when others are free to explore new perspectives. Of course, there is no magic mechanism to bring this about. The simplest way to encourage others to open their hearts and minds is for our hearts and minds to be open, believing in our own potential to learn and grow. I believe sincerity and humility are imperative for advocates, because no one has all the answers.

Recognizing this, I worked for years to set aside everything I thought I "knew" in order to find what is fundamentally important. I now realize that virtually all our actions can be traced to two drives: a desire for fulfillment and happiness, and a need to avoid or alleviate suffering. At the core, something is "good" if it leads to more happiness, and something is "bad" if it leads to more suffering. This may seem simplistic at first, but it really does allow us to cut through confusion, providing a straightforward measure by which to judge the consequences of our actions and evaluate our advocacy.

In his book *Painism: A Modern Morality*, Richard Ryder points out, "At its extreme, pain is more powerful than pleasure can ever be. Pain overrules pleasure within the individual far more effectively than pleasure can dominate pain." Because of this, I believe that reducing suffering is the ultimate good, and must be our bottom line.

PRINCIPLES OF ADVOCACY

If you are reading this, you are obviously concerned about more than just your own immediate pleasure. The question then is, How can we best make a difference in a world where suffering is so widespread?

A basic understanding of human nature shows that all of us have an affinity for the known and immediate. Most people working for a better world concentrate on those closest to them, geographically or biologically. Even those who look beyond species often focus on either the familiar or the fantastic, with a majority of resources spent on cats and dogs, endangered species, or campaigns focused on high-profile animals. Furthermore, we all want to feel that our efforts have accomplished something concrete, that we've been "victorious." It often doesn't matter how significant the accomplishment is, or even if the world is truly better off, but only that something tangible has been achieved.

Taking into account these predispositions and our bottom line of reducing suffering has led Vegan Outreach to formulate two guiding principles to maximize the amount of good we can accomplish:

Set Aside Personal Biases

Rather than focusing on what appeals to (or offends) us personally, we challenge ourselves to approach advocacy through a straightforward analysis of the world as it is, striving solely to alleviate as much suffering as possible.

Recognize Our Severely Limited Resources and Time

It is an inescapable fact: When we choose to do one thing, we are choosing not to do another. There is no way around it. Instead of choosing to "do something, do anything," we challenge ourselves to pursue actions that will likely lead to the greatest reduction in suffering.

WHY VEGAN OUTREACH?

Based on these two principles, Vegan Outreach seeks to expose the cruelties of factory farms and industrial slaughterhouses while providing honest information on how to make cruelty-free choices. Our emphasis on ethical eating is derived from our principles of advocacy, not vice versa. No philosophy, lifestyle, or diet has any value in and of itself. Rather, the significance of promoting cruelty-free eating is that it allows us to alleviate as much suffering as possible, for three reasons:

The Numbers

Ninety-nine of every one hundred animals killed annually in the United States are slaughtered for human consumption. That comes to nine billion land animals—far more than the world's entire human population—raised and killed for food each year in this country alone.

The Suffering

If these billions of animals lived happy, healthy lives and

had quick and painless deaths, then a concern for suffering would lead us to focus our efforts elsewhere. But animals raised for food must endure horrible cruelties. Perhaps the most difficult aspect of advocating on behalf of these animals is trying to describe the suffering they endure: the confinement and overcrowding, the stench, the racket, the extremes of heat and cold, the attacks and even cannibalism, the hunger and starvation, the illness, the mutilation, the broken bones and failing organs, etc. Indeed, every year, hundreds of millions of animals—many times more than the number killed for fur, in shelters, and in laboratories combined—don't even make it to slaughter. They actually suffer to death.

The Opportunity

If there were nothing we could do about these animals' suffering—if it all happened in a distant land beyond our influence—then, again, our focus would be different. But exposing factory farming and advocating ethical eating is, by far, our best option for making a better world. We don't have to overthrow a government. We don't have to forsake modern life. We don't have to win an election or convince Congress of the validity of our argument. We don't have to start a group or organize a campaign. Rather, every day, every single person makes decisions that affect the lives of farmed animals. Informing and inspiring people to open their hearts and minds to making compassionate choices leads to many fewer animals suffering.

Nearly everyone wants a better world. We oppose injustice and violence and wish we could do something to stop it. What can we do about starvation and AIDS in sub-Saharan Africa? We can donate money, write letters, or try to get the government to intervene and give more aid. All of those efforts, though well meaning, are often far removed from having a proportionate or long-term impact.

Focused, effective animal advocacy, however, allows us to have an immediate and profound influence every single day. Preventing animals from being bred for factory farms may not appear to be a particularly exciting or inspiring goal, especially compared to the plight of individual animals or the urgency of the latest tragedy. But if we are to alleviate as much suffering as possible, we need to maximize our impact: Through vegetarian advocacy, every single person we meet is a potential victory!

VARIATIONS ON A THEME

The logic outlined on the preceding pages seems straightforward to me now, but I didn't arrive at these conclusions overnight. Before founding Vegan Outreach and seeking to maximize our impact, Jack Norris and I followed the "do something, do anything" philosophy, trying to fight many different forms of animal exploitation through various methods of advocacy—from letter writing campaigns to scores of protests and everything in between, including civil disobedience.

Even within the realm of exposing factory farms and promoting vegetarianism, there are many different options. Vegan Outreach seeks to reach as many new people as possible with our illustrated booklets, which provide detailed and documented accounts of the realities of modern agribusiness, along with honest and useful information about making compassionate choices. Similarly, the Christian Vegetarian Association's booklet *Would Jesus Eat Meat Today?* reaches out to many people through their existing ethical framework. This allows CVA to advocate to a vast audience for whom other approaches may be less effective.

Others focus on harnessing the power of video footage. Certain groups take out free spots on public access TV; others, like Compassion Over Killing, air commercials. The Internet also offers many advocacy opportunities. Different regional groups provide important resources and information, from publishing local shopping and dining guides to organizing social gatherings and building supportive communities.

We need everyone's efforts if we are going to bring about change as quickly as possible. There is much to do: We must reach and influence those who might be willing to go vegan; reach and influence those who might be willing to go vegetarian; reach and influence those who won't (now) go veg, but who might eat fewer animals or stop buying meat from factory farms—and support all these people as they continue to learn and grow.

Outreach to each of these audiences is necessary if we are to help a large and diverse society evolve to a new ethical norm. No single tactic or message will be optimally effective for everyone. This is why Vegan Outreach produces a range of literature. With these tools, anyone, in any situation, can be a highly effective advocate for the animals.

ADVOCACY FOR MAXIMUM CHANGE

Vegan Outreach works for maximum change—the greatest reduction in suffering per dollar donated and hour worked—by presenting the optimal message to our target audience. Of course, with an infinite budget we could provide a customized message to everyone. Given our limited resources, though, Vegan Outreach focuses on young adults—particularly college students—for three main reasons:

The Relative Willingness and Ability to Change

Obviously, not every young adult is willing to stop eating meat. But relative to the population as a whole, this age group tends to be more open-minded and in a position where they aren't as restricted by parents, tradition, habits, etc.

The Full Impact of Change

Even if young people and senior citizens were equally likely to change, over the course of their lives, youth can save more animals. They not only have more meals ahead of them, but also more opportunities to influence others.

The Ability to Reach Large Numbers

Whether on a college campus or outside a concert, for a relatively small investment of time, an activist can hand an *Even If You Like Meat* or *Compassionate Choices* to hundreds of young people who otherwise might have never viewed a full and compelling case for compassion.

Choosing the optimal message is vital. Some argue

that we should appeal to self-interest by attributing great health benefits to a vegan diet. But consider, for example, how much money and time respected health organizations have spent on the ineffectual campaign to convince people to simply add more fruits and vegetables to their diets. Furthermore, claims that veganism prevents or reverses heart disease or that meat causes colon cancer can be met not only with examples of vegans who died of those diseases, but with counterclaims that soy causes breast cancer, that the Atkins diet has been proven superior, or that people with a certain blood type can't be vegetarian. No matter the underlying truth, the public will believe the claims that support the status quo and the path of least resistance.

Of course, if you were to ask the average individual what is important, personal health would come before factory farming. As advocates, however, we're not trying to reinforce people's existing concerns and prejudices. Rather, our goal is to reveal hidden truths and have people open their hearts and minds to the idea of expanding their circle of consideration. Although more people turn away from graphic pictures than from graphs of heart attack statistics or relative water usage, it isn't because the former is the "wrong" message. Rather, unlike abstract statistics of waste production or cancer rates, revelations of obvious cruelty cannot be debated, ignored, or forgotten; they have a personal, emotional impact and demand a real response.

Exposing what goes on in factory farms and slaughterhouses surely won't persuade everyone at this time. But it is far better if only some open their minds to change than if all politely nod in agreement as they continue on to McDonald's for a "healthy" chicken salad.

Despite the efforts of thousands of people over the course of decades, trying to appeal to everyone hasn't worked. It's well past time to give up the idea that there is some perfect, noncontroversial, self-centered argument that will magically inspire everyone to go vegan.

If our goal is to advocate for the animals, that's what we should do—because it works! Pointing out that factory farming causes unnecessary suffering is honest, straightforward, and the only argument people can't refute or nitpick. Showing people the plight of farmed animals is a highly effective means of creating fundamental, lasting change. Again and again, revealing factory farming's hidden but undeniable cruelty has proven the most compelling reason for changing one's diet—and maintaining that change—in the face of peer pressure, tradition, the latest fad, etc.

Every year, Vegan Outreach's hundreds of leafleters find increased interest in our message. We regularly receive feedback like, "I had no idea what went on! Thank you so much for opening my eyes!"

Because of our efforts at exposing the animals' plight, awareness is growing: Factory farms—unknown to most people only two decades ago—are now commonly condemned as ethical abominations, with reforms slowly abolishing the most egregious abuses. And since 2006— the first year Vegan Outreach distributed over a million booklets—fewer animals are being killed for food in the United States!

And yet, there are many more people to reach. The simplest way to get information to people is to stock displays of Vegan Outreach literature at libraries, music and bookstores, co-ops and natural food shops, coffeehouses, and sympathetic restaurants.

Youth, though, is where the animals get the biggest bang for the buck. Vegan Outreach's Adopt a College program (adoptacollege.org), a network of activists leafleting local campuses (and concerts and other venues), serves to reach out methodically to our prime audience. This is the first systematic, nationwide plan to create maximum change by taking the animals' plight to the most receptive people. We know this works, and you can join the others who are part of this powerful, efficient, effective activism. You don't need to start a group, or publish a Web site, or organize anything. You just need to devote some of your time or money to making a difference. We'll provide all the materials and guidance you need. Going out to leaflet for the first time might seem intimidating, but most activists get over their nervousness once they hand out their first few booklets. They'll also tell you how rewarding leafleting can be. Vegan Outreach is often able to put new activists in touch with experienced leafleters, which can make it even easier to get started.

Being a part of Vegan Outreach will vastly increase your ability to make a difference. Whether you leaflet or finance the distribution of our booklets, for every person you help convince to go vegetarian, you double the impact of your life's choices. If, for example, you provide booklets to fifty new people tomorrow and just one decides to go vegetarian, you will have changed that person's life forever. More importantly, you'll have saved, with just a small investment of time or money, as many animals as you'll save with every food choice you make during the rest of your life!

In other words, if we agree that being vegetarian is vital, then we must recognize that taking part in effective animal advocacy is many, many times more important.

EFFECTIVE ADVOCACY = FOCUS

Anyone who has been vegetarian for more than a few minutes knows the many roadblocks—habit, tradition, convenience, taste, familiarity, peer pressure, etc.—that keep people from considering the animals' plight. Many people are looking for an excuse to dismiss us. Knowing this, we can't give anyone any reason to ignore the terrible and unnecessary suffering on factory farms and in slaughterhouses.

If we want to be as effective as we possibly can be for the animals, it is essential that we recognize and avoid common traps. Remember: Our message is simple. We shouldn't distract people by offering every piece of information that strikes us as somewhat anti-meat. Nor should we try to address every tangential argument, letting our discussions degrade into debates over Jesus' loaves and fishes, abortion, politics, desert islands, evolution, Grandpa's cholesterol level, etc. Nothing can counter the fact that eating animals causes unnecessary suffering.

Similarly, we can't afford to build our case from questionable sources. Factory farms and slaughterhouses are hidden from view, and the industry's PR machine denies the inherent cruelties ("Animals are treated well; slaughterhouses are strictly regulated"). The public won't believe otherwise just because we say so. We must present them with well-documented information—from industry sources or respected, nonpartisan third parties—and indisputable photos and videos.

It's also extremely important to consider how the public will respond to certain information. No matter how reasonable or powerful a claim may seem to us, and no matter how we think the public should react, we can't make claims that may be "misinterpreted." Even those from highly regarded sources can have disastrous repercussions. Health or environmental claims that primarily denigrate beef or red meat, for example, are often taken by the public as a reason to eat more chickens.

Our focus must remain on the animals, not ourselves or our particular diets. Our choices don't need to be defended; our lifestyle is not an end in itself. Living ethically is not about following a dogma, nor is it about avoiding a list of forbidden ingredients. It is only a tool for opposing cruelty and reducing suffering. Remember, our goal is not to express our rage at animal abuse, or show how much we know. We don't want to "win an argument with a meat eater." We want people to open their hearts and minds to the animals' plight. It all simplifies to this:

- Buying meat, eggs, and dairy causes unnecessary suffering.
- Each one of us can choose not to cause this suffering.

STAYING HEALTHY

While leafleting colleges across the country in the mid-1990s, Jack was often told, "I was veg for a while, but I didn't feel healthy." This real-world feedback, still heard by leafleters today, stands in stark contrast to the "vegetarianism is a wonder diet/meat is a deadly poison" message favored by some activists.

Even a moderate health argument doesn't hold sway over most people—especially young people. But the health argument is worse than an inefficient use of our limited resources. When we recite amazing claims, the public often hears it as dishonest propaganda. This ultimately hurts animals, because most people will then dismiss all animal advocates. Those few who do try a vegetarian diet because of its purported "magical properties" will likely quit if they don't immediately lose weight, increase their energy, etc. They will then tell everyone how awful they felt as a vegetarian, and how much better they feel now as a meat eater. Just one failed vegetarian can counter the efforts of many advocates.

The nutritional case historically presented by vegetarians was so bad that, in 2001, Jack became a registered dietitian in order to evaluate nutrition research firsthand and provide sound recommendations. If we want to do our best to prevent suffering, we must learn and provide a complete, unbiased summary of the nutritional aspects of an ethical diet, including uncertainties and potential concerns. Doing so leads people to realize we are not simply partisan propagandists, and it creates healthy spokespeople for the animals!

COUNTERING THE STEREOTYPE

Society's stereotype of animal advocates and vegans is a significant roadblock to widespread change. The word "vegan" rarely needs to be explained anymore; but unfortunately, some still use it as shorthand for one who is deprived, fanatical, and antisocial. This caricature guarantees that veganism won't be considered—let alone adopted—on a wide scale.

Regrettably, the "angry vegan" image has some basis in reality. Not only have I known many obsessive, misanthropic vegans, I was also one myself. My anger and self-righteousness gave many people a lifetime excuse to ignore the realities hidden behind their food choices.

As a reaction to what goes on in factory farms and slaughterhouses, very strong feelings, such as revulsion and outrage, are understandable and entirely justified. The question, though, isn't what is warranted, but rather, what helps animals. I have known hundreds of outraged activists who insisted, "Animal liberation by any means necessary! I'm willing to do anything!" Yet few of these people are still working toward animal liberation today.

If we truly want to have a fundamental, lasting impact on the world, we must deal with our emotions in a constructive way. We need to ask ourselves the following:

- Are we willing to direct our passion, rather than have it rule us?
- Are we willing to put the animals' interests before our personal desires?
- Are we willing to focus seriously and systematically on effective advocacy?

It is not enough to be a vegan, or even a dedicated vegan advocate. We must remember the bottom line—reducing suffering—and actively be the opposite of the vegan stereotype. Just as we need everyone to look beyond the short-term satisfaction of following habits and traditions, we need to move past our sorrow and anger to optimal advocacy. We must learn "how to win friends and influence people," so that we leave everyone we meet with the impression of a joyful individual leading a fulfilling and meaningful life.

AN ACTIVIST'S LIFE = A MEANINGFUL LIFE

I'm not saying we should put on an act of being happy. Rather, as thoughtful activists, we can truly *be* happy!

Looking at the long arc of history, we see how much society has advanced in just the last few centuries. It was over two thousand years ago that the ideals of democracy were first proposed in ancient Greece, but only during the eighteenth century did humanity see even the beginnings of a truly democratic system. Not until late in the nineteenth century was slavery officially abolished in the developed world. In all of human history, only in the last hundred years was child labor abolished in the developed world, child abuse criminalized, women given the vote, and minorities given more rights.

Many people worked diligently to bring about those ethical advances for humanity. Because of the number of individuals suffering and the reason for this hidden brutality, I believe animal liberation is the moral imperative of our time. If we take suffering seriously and commit to optimal advocacy, we too can bring about fundamental change. We can already see progress in just the past decade—public concern for farmed animals' interests and condemnation of factory farms, as well as more vegetarians, near-vegetarians, and vegetarian products. Our advocacy's focus, tools, and programs have also improved immensely during that time—Vegan Outreach's Adopt a College program, for example, was only launched in 2003.

Animal liberation can be the future. As the magazine *The Economist* concluded,

> Historically, man has expanded the reach of his ethical calculations, as ignorance and want have receded, first beyond family and tribe, later beyond religion, race, and nation.
>
> To bring other species more fully into the range of these decisions may seem unthinkable to moderate opinion now. One day, decades or centuries hence, it may seem no more than "civilized" behavior requires.[1]

We can be the generation to bring about this next great ethical advance. We should revel in the freedom and opportunity we have to be part of something so profound, something fundamentally good. This is as meaningful and joyous a life as I can imagine!

Fewer than four hundred years ago, the Inquisition sentenced Galileo to prison for pointing out that the Earth is not the center of the physical universe. With our

---

1 *The Economist*, "What Humans Owe to Animals," August 19, 1995.

efforts, society will recognize that humans are not the center of the moral universe, and will look back with horror and disgust on the subjugation of animals for food. This century can be the one in which society stops torturing and slaughtering our fellow earthlings for a fleeting taste of flesh.

It is up to us to make this happen.

We have no excuse for waiting—we have the knowledge, the tools, and the truth. Taking a stand against cruelty to animals requires only our choice.

To paraphrase Martin Luther King, Jr.:

> The arc of history is long
>> And ragged
>> And often unclear
> But ultimately
> It progresses toward justice.

We can each be a part of that progress!

In the end, in our hearts, we know that, regardless of what we think of ourselves, our actions reveal the kind of person we really are. We each determine our life's narrative. We can, like most, choose to allow the narrative to be imposed on us, mindlessly accept the current default, follow the crowd, and take whatever we can.

Or we can choose to actively author our lives, and live with a larger purpose, dedicated to a better world for all. We can choose to be extraordinary!

The choice is fundamental.

The choice is vital.

And the choice is ours, today.

Bibliography

Ball, Matt, and Bruce Friedrich. *The Animal Activist's Handbook: Maximizing Our Positive Impact in Today's World*. Brooklyn, NY: Lantern Books, 2009.

Farm to Fridge. Video created by Mercy for Animals, narrated by James Cromwell.

Foer, Jonathan Safran. *Eating Animals*. New York: Little, Brown and Company, 2009.

Haidt, Jonathan. *The Happiness Hypothesis: Finding Modern Truth in Ancient Wisdom*. Cambridge, MA: Perseus Books, 2006.

Heath, Chip, and Dan Heath. *Switch: How to Change Things When Change Is Hard*. New York: Crown, 2010.

Marcus, Erik. *Meat Market: Animals, Ethics, and Money*. Minneapolis, MN: Brio Press, 2005.

Meet Your Meat. Video created by People for the Ethical Treatment of Animals (PETA), narrated by Alec Baldwin, and directed by Bruce Friedrich and Cem Akin.

Norris, Jack, and Virginia Messina. *Vegan for Life: Everything You Need to Know to Be Healthy and Fit on a Plant-Based Diet*. Cambridge, MA: Da Capo Press, 2011.

Norwood, F. Bailey, and Jayson L. Lusk. *Compassion,*

by the Pound: The Economics of Farm Animal Welfare. New York: Oxford University Press, 2011.

Proulx, E. Annie. *That Old Ace in the Hole*. New York: Scribner, 2002.

Ryder, Richard D. *Painism: A Modern Morality*. London: Open Gate Press, 2003.

Singer, Peter. *How Are We to Live?: Ethics in an Age of Self-Interest*. Amherst, NY: Prometheus Books, 1995.

———. *Practical Ethics*. New York: Cambridge University Press, 1980.

The Witness. Video directed by Jenny Stein and produced by James LaVeck (Tribe of Heart, 2000).

Wheelan, Charles. *Naked Statistics: Stripping the Dread from the Data*. New York: W. W. Norton, 2013.

About the Authors

MATT BALL co-founded Vegan Outreach in 1993. He is the co-author, with Bruce Friedrich, of *The Animal Activist's Handbook: Maximizing Our Positive Impact in Today's World* (Lantern, 2009). He was inducted into the Animal Rights Hall of Fame in 2005.

PETER SINGER is currently the Ira W. DeCamp Professor of Bioethics at Princeton University and the author, among many other books, of *Animal Liberation and How Are We to Live?*

PAUL SHAPIRO is Vice-President, Farm Animal Protection, at The Humane Society of the United States.

ANNE GREEN was Vegan Outreach's founding Vice President, and served as Vegan Outreach's Director of Programs and Development.

About the Publisher

LANTERN BOOKS was founded in 1999 on the principle of living with a greater depth and commitment to the preservation of the natural world. In addition to publishing books on animal advocacy, vegetarianism, religion, and environmentalism, Lantern is dedicated to printing books in the U.S. on recycled paper and saving resources in day-to-day operations. Lantern is honored to be a recipient of the highest standard in environmentally responsible publishing from the Green Press Initiative.

www.lanternbooks.com

CPSIA information can be obtained at www.ICGtesting.com
Printed in the USA
BVOW07s2001210814

363671BV00001B/1/P